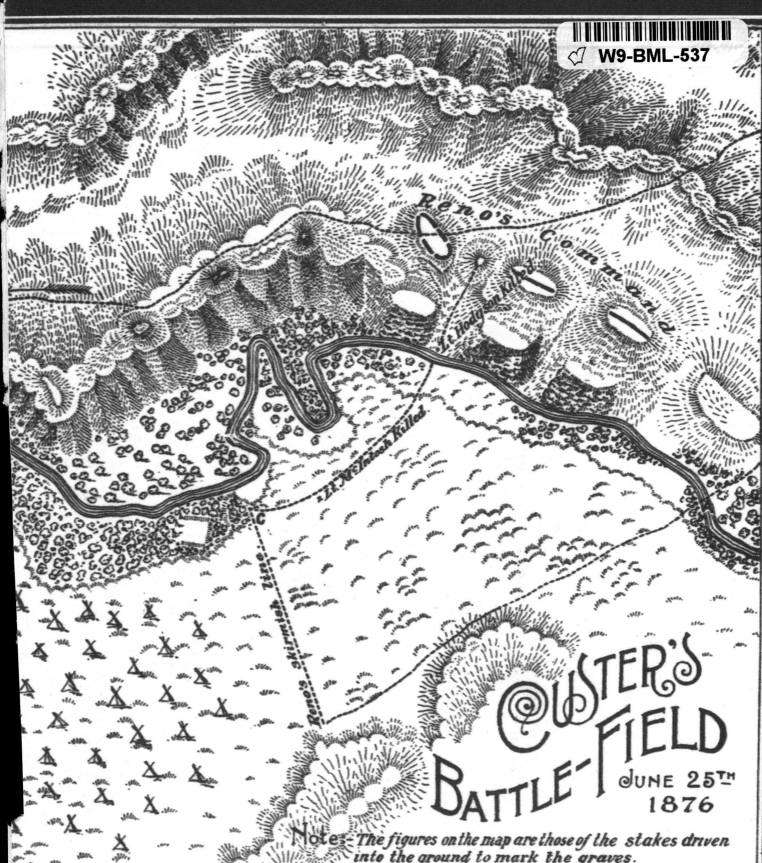

Reno's Command

Lt. Hodgson Killed

Lt. McIntosh Killed

Reno's Skirmish Line

Custer's Battle-Field
June 25th 1876

Note:— The figures on the map are those of the stakes driven
into the ground to mark the graves.

1 Capt. M.W. Keogh	7th Cav.	
2		
3 Lieut. J Calhoun.	7th Cav.	
4 Lieut. J.J. Crittenden.	20th Inf.	
5 Lt.Col. G.A. Custer.	7th Cav.	
6 Capt. T.W. Custer.	7th Cav.	
7 Capt. G.W. Yates.	7th Cav.	
8 Lieut. W. Van W. Reily.	7th Cav	
9 Lieut. A.E. Smith.	7th Cav.	
10 Lieut. W.W. Cooke.	7th Cav	
11 Mr. W.B. Custer		
12 Mr Reed.		

HARPER'S WEEKLY.

A
JOURNAL OF CIVILIZATION.

VOL. VIII.—No. 377.]   NEW YORK, SATURDAY, MARCH 19, 1864.   [$1,00 FOR FOUR MONTHS. / $3,00 PER YEAR IN ADVANCE.

Entered according to Act of Congress, in the Year 1864, by Harper & Brothers, in the Clerk's Office of the District Court for the Southern District of New York.

BRIGADIER-GENERAL GEORGE A. CUSTER.—Photographed by Brady.—[See Page 187.]

Facing page: **Indian Casualties at Little Bighorn**
Minneconjou warrior Red Horse drew a series of pictographs based on his remembrances of the Little Bighorn battle. He created the drawings in 1881 at the request of an army surgeon stationed at the Cheyenne River Agency in Dakota Territory.

And he never stopped being a boy. He was devoted to his family and especially his mother: He would cry whenever he left her and had to be pulled away from her embrace. He surrounded himself with close friends, relatives, and household members in an attempt to approximate the full and happy Custer home of his childhood. Though he was often cold and distant with officers and men under his command, he could be as playful as a pup with good friends and family. He often saw the world through the innocent eyes of a youth who had spent far too much time reading of romantic heroes and dashing deeds. The pursuit of glory through war was, he thought, life's most exalted activity, and he never felt more alive than when in the midst of battle. "If there was any poetry or romance in war he could develop it," said General Phil Sheridan, his commander and friend of many years. And Custer had the peculiar gift of ignoring war's horrors when they intruded upon his rose-colored dream. He felt himself a direct descendant of Caesar's centurion, Tennyson's knight, and Scott's cavalier, and the image of the *beau sabreur* he cultivated was embraced by the American public.

Custer was, above all, fearless in battle. This more than anything accounts for his lightning-quick rise in rank during the Civil War to brevet major general, one of the fastest series of promotions in American military history. Custer's West Point class of 1862 requested and was granted an early graduation, in June 1861. When Custer and his thirty-three classmates received their diplomas, each was granted the rank of lieutenant. Three and a half years later, in October 1864, he was brevetted to major general of volunteers at the age of twenty-four, the youngest man ever to hold that rank in U.S. Army history. There were several other "boy generals"—Ranald Mackenzie and

General Winfield Scott

General Winfield Scott and Staff

"Old Fuss and Feathers," second from right, was the oldest and most respected military advisor to President Abraham Lincoln. He was also one of the few who predicted the Civil War would last for many years. Scott and his staff were pictured in Washington, D. C., in July 1861.

graduation, he had been Officer of the Guard at the summer camp. That night at dusk he failed to break up a fight between two cadets, instead declaring, "Let's have a fair fight." By the time the pair separated, two academy officials were on the scene. The next morning Custer was placed under arrest for neglect of duty and "conduct to the prejudice of good order and military discipline." At the court-martial on July 5, he pled guilty. Despite a character reference from the Officer of the Day and testimony from all concerned that the matter was trivial in every respect, Custer was found guilty on both counts. Ten days later the sentence was released: Owing to the intercession of Congressman Bingham and probably the West Point "good old boy" network in Washington, Custer was merely given a reprimand, and told to report immediately to the nation's capital. He hopped on a steamer on July 18 bound for New York City. Arriving that afternoon, he bought a lieutenant's uniform, a Colt pistol, spurs, and a sword at Horstmann's, the famous military outfitter. He had his picture taken for his sister Lydia, then caught a night train for Washington.

The young lieutenant reported for duty at the War Department on July 20, 1861. The officer on duty, about to deliver Custer's assignment papers, suddenly asked him, for no good reason, if he would like to meet General Winfield Scott. The hero of the Mexican War and a soldier for more than half a century, "Old Fuss and Feathers," at seventy-five, was no longer a field commander. But the nation's most respected soldier was President Lincoln's chief military advisor, and one of the few realists who warned that the Civil War would drag on for years.

Custer was ushered into Scott's office, a makeshift War Room filled with officers and congressmen studying a map of the Bull Run

Above: **General Pierre G. T. Beauregard**
Beauregard led the Confederate army that routed the Army of the Potomac in the first major battle of the war, in the Bull Run River country of Virginia on July 21, 1861.

Left: **Major General George B. McClellan**
McClellan was appointed by Lincoln to command the Army of the Potomac after the disaster at Bull Run. He eventually added Custer to his personal staff. Custer always remained loyal to "Little Mac," and was later known as a McClellan man, which eventually caused him political problems when McClellan disagreed with the president's Republican policies.

River country of Virginia, where the two armies were about to clash. The cordial Scott asked the dazzled lieutenant about his orders, and whether he preferred an assignment in Washington or to report to his assigned unit, the Second Cavalry, stationed near Bull Run under the command of General Irvin McDowell. Custer stammered that he desired to join his company at once, with the hope of participating in the battle. Scott commended him, then told him to find a horse and return early that evening, as he had dispatches to be delivered to McDowell. Was Custer afraid of a night ride? No, sir.

Union Army Camp
McClellan's army spent much of its winter in early 1862 training and drilling in camp.

Airborne Reconnaissance
Professor Thaddeus Lowe invented, and demonstrated here, a gas-filled balloon for the Union army. On May 4, 1862, while attached to the Topographical Engineers, Custer observed the enemy withdrawal from Yorktown while suspended from the balloon.

He spent the next few hours visiting the largest livery stables in the city in search of a mount. There was none to be found. He was on the brink of despair when, on Pennsylvania Avenue, he ran into an enlisted man formerly stationed at West Point. He too was assigned to McDowell's army, and here was another stroke of Custer's Luck: The soldier was in the capital to pick up an extra horse left by his battery upon their departure from the city. The horse, named Wellington, had also been assigned to the academy, and Custer had ridden him many times. The soldier offered the use of Wellington, and after Custer picked up Scott's dispatches, they were off.

After riding twenty-five miles, they arrived at Centreville, Virginia, about three in the morning, picking their way among fifty regiments of sleeping soldiers along miles of road. Custer delivered the papers, saw to his mount, and washed down a quick meal of steak and cornbread with black coffee. Then he bridled his horse and set out in search of his unit, the Second Cavalry. Just before dawn, he found the column of horses. He reported for duty, met his fellow officers, and learned of the battle plans. His regiment was to be part of a flank attack on the enemy's left while half the army, two divisions, drove straight across the steep-banked creek.

At dawn the army of volunteers marched into battle against the Confederates led by General Pierre Gustave Toutant Beauregard. Custer's unit was assigned to guard the artillery. Out of range on a ridge above the battery, he had his first view of men at war. He and his fellow cavalrymen were eager to engage the enemy, now retreating before the Union army. Victory seemed to be at hand. But when the Confederates counterflanked the Federals, the green troops broke and ran back across the creek. Abandoned artillery, muskets, flags, and band instruments littered the battlefield. "Officers and men joined in one vast crowd," Custer wrote later in his memoirs, "abandoning, except in isolated instances, all attempts to preserve their organizations." He and his company, among the last troops to leave the field, were told to ride back to Centreville, where they waited for hours until ordered to return to Washington.

The First Battle of Bull Run was finished, and the field was Beauregard's. In a dreary rain, Custer and his men rode their tired mounts twenty-five long miles. In Washington, he dismounted and fell asleep under a tree in the downpour. He woke up stiff and sore.

His first taste of battle had been less than glorious, but the young lieutenant was smitten. He had embarked on a love affair that would last a lifetime.

The rout at Bull Run cost McDowell his position as Lincoln appointed Major General George Brinton McClellan to take over command of the Army of the Potomac. A West Pointer from the class of '46, McClellan had forged a distinguished career in the army and was a revered commander. Recognizing the lack of proper training and discipline among the volunteer troops, McClellan reorganized the army. Custer's Second Cavalry became the Fifth, attached to the brigade of Brigadier General Philip Kearny, a professional soldier of fortune who had lost an arm in the Mexican War. Kearny, a strict disciplinarian, had volunteered after Bull Run. He drilled his troops constantly, and under him Custer learned the importance of discipline—especially after participating in a botched midnight raid that turned into a full-scale retreat.

Custer was reassigned after an order was issued forbidding regular army officers from serving under volunteer officers. There followed a four-month leave of absence due to an unspecified illness. He spent most of his time in Monroe, where he noticed the pretty nineteen-year-old daughter of Judge Daniel Stanton Bacon. The Bacons were one of the town's upper-class families. Elizabeth, or "Libbie," was not impressed by Custer, particularly when he staggered roaring drunk past her house in plain sight of her entire family. Some good ultimately came out of the episode: After a stern talking-to from sister Lydia, he never touched alcohol again.

During his leave, Custer also visited his parents' new home, an eighty-acre farm they had recently moved to in northwestern Ohio. Younger brothers Nevin and Boston were helping their father, but sixteen-year-old Tom had enlisted as a private in the Twenty-First Ohio Infantry a month before. He was still following in his big brother's footsteps.

When Custer returned to the army in February, he found a steadily growing mass of volunteers that was slowly learning to soldier. McClellan's command decisions had been for the most part well-advised, though "Little Mac" erred on the side of caution as he was determined to have a well-trained army before joining battle again. Lieutenant Custer hadn't missed any action in the Virginia area. For a month, his

"Officers and men joined in one vast crowd, abandoning, except in isolated instances, all attempts to preserve their organizations."
—Custer, writing of the First Battle of Bull Run

Invasion of the Virginia Peninsula

Union troops land on the Virginia Peninsula in spring 1862. McClellan's plan to fight his way up the peninsula to Richmond was ingenious, but its execution was muddled and the campaign petered out after six months.

duty was routine, drilling by day and socializing by night. When the rebel forces around Centreville abruptly retreated south in fear of an expected attack by McClellan that never came, the cavalry was ordered to trail them for information. Custer's horsemen ran into the Confederate rear guard, and when the order came to drive back the enemy pickets, Custer volunteered his troop.

In his first charge at the head of a cavalry troop, Custer was admirable. His men galloped up and over a hill with sabers held high, and drove the pickets back across a creek to the larger Confederate force. Satisfied, Custer and his men returned to their column, the only casualty a soldier with a scratched head.

A few weeks later, McClellan's grand plan was put into action. More than 100,000 men aboard 400 vessels of every shape and size were shuttled 200 miles down the Potomac River in twenty days to advance on Richmond, Virginia, from the east. The armada disembarked at Fortress Monroe, on the tip of the Virginia Peninsula. Early in April, they laid siege to Yorktown, twenty miles up the York River, where Custer came under fire twice during reconnaissance missions.

A short time later, he was assigned to the army's topographical engineers unit, busy constructing a line of fortifications near Yorktown. He was chosen to go aloft in a gas-buoyed balloon to reconnoiter

Crossing the Chickahominy

A. R. Waud's sketch of Custer crossing the Chickahominy River on May 22, 1862. The river was swollen by spring rains, and Custer received much attention for his bravery by wading into the rushing water to test its depth. During a skirmish two days later, he was the first to lead his unit across the river and the last man to return.

the Confederate positions. These recently developed balloons came into use for the first time during this campaign and proved valuable for intelligence gathering. Custer sat in a basket below the balloon as it slowly rose into the sky. When the balloon, restrained by a ground crew holding onto ropes, reached 1,000 feet, Custer, aided by field glasses, sketched the enemy fortifications and took notes. Early in the morning of May 4, 1862, he viewed the Confederates withdrawing from Yorktown. The news was telegraphed to McClellan, and Custer and another officer volunteered to be the first to gallop across the river and into the enemy sector. The army followed Custer, and soon the entire column was marching up the peninsula in pursuit of the rebels.

The Federals caught up with the Confederates at Williamsburg early the next morning. The young lieutenant rode ahead of his column, engaging in skirmishes and dodging sniper bullets. At Skiff Creek, he found the bridge on fire and stamped the flames out; the column was able to cross the bridge, and his commanding officer, General William F. "Baldy" Smith, cited him for gallantry. It would be the first of many citations.

Smith then assigned Custer to the brigade of Brigadier General Winfield Scott Hancock, an aggressive leader and one of the best generals in the Union army. With Custer helping to guide them, the brigade crossed several dams and closed to within a mile of the rebel position's flank by mid-afternoon. While Hancock's brigade was waiting for further orders, a Confederate brigade began a ragged charge. Custer galloped to the front of the Union line and led the counterattack, and a sea of bayonets routed the enemy. Hancock's victory was one of the keys to the battle, and he recognized Custer with his second citation of the day.

The army marched slowly up the peninsula through the Virginia countryside. On May 20, it reached the swollen Chickahominy River, the last natural barrier before Richmond some twenty miles away, and found all its bridges burned. The next several days were spent investigating the best crossing sites. Custer accompanied the army's chief engineer and attracted attention by fearlessly wading into the river on several occasions to test the depth. A few days later he was involved in a skirmish near New Bridge when a force of Union infantry and cavalry forded the river and clashed with a rebel detachment. Custer was the first across the river and the last to return.

Presidential Visit

On October 3, 1862, President Abraham Lincoln visited Union troops after the Battle of Antietam. Captain Custer stands alone on the far right. This is the only photograph of Lincoln and Custer together.

THE POLITICS OF SLAVERY

Though there were other issues that divided America in the decades leading up to the Civil War, slavery was the most incendiary. Tensions between the slave-holding and "free" regions of the United States had risen steadily since the Revolution, but few thought the issue should be allowed to destroy the Union, and many hoped it would die a natural death.

Astute observers realized early on that the future of slavery would be decided not by those states where it already existed, but by those new states carved out of the vast territory to the west and the voting power they wielded. In 1820, when there were eleven free states and eleven slave states, Congress admitted Maine as a free state. Southern objections to this led to the Missouri Compromise, wherein Missouri would be allowed to enter the Union as a slave state. At the same time, Congress drew a line through the remaining territory of the Louisiana Purchase and barred slavery north of that line. That would be the end of it, thought some.

But heated discussion and occasional action over the issue increased, and the inadequacies of that simplistic solution were soon apparent, especially after the annexation of Texas and the acquisition of new territory following the Mexican War. The Great Compromise of 1850, largely engineered by Senator Henry Clay of Kentucky, permitted California to enter the Union as a free state while at the same time strengthening the Fugitive Slave Act. Its passage put off violence for a decade.

But tensions continued to mount. Harriet Beecher Stowe's *Uncle Tom's Cabin*, published in 1852, persuaded millions of readers throughout the world of slavery's horrors and acted as a lightning rod for the "peculiar institution's" enemies. When Democrat Stephen A. Douglas of Illinois pushed through the Kansas-Nebraska Act of 1854, which allowed the residents of those new territories to decide for themselves on the slavery issue within their borders, many in the North were outraged that slavery might be allowed in an area previously thought to be free forever.

The political result was the new Republican Party, which owed its formation to Northern protests against the Kansas-Nebraska Act. The party attracted Free Soil and antislavery adherents, and also many Northern Democrats and remnants of the tattered Whig Party. The party gained in numbers steadily through the 1856 and 1858 elections. The Dred Scott Decision of 1857 (which ruled that slaves were not citizens, and that Congress could not prohibit slavery in territories) and John Brown's ill-fated 1858 slave rebellion (put down by a young cavalry officer named Robert E. Lee) polarized allegiances even more.

Then, in 1860, the Republican Party nominated a compromise candidate, a former congressman of moderate antislavery views named Abraham Lincoln, to face the dominant Democrats. The Democratic Party, the party of George Armstrong Custer and his father, had evolved from the political organization that Andrew Jackson put together when he won the presidency in 1828. During the next thirty years, Democrats usually controlled both the presidency and Congress. Initially the party had espoused states' rights and limited government, but slavery splintered the party into Northern and Southern wings. In 1860, the Northerners nominated Stephen A. Douglas, while the Southerners nominated John C. Breckinridge. This allowed Lincoln, the Republican candidate in the party's first presidential campaign, to gain the presidency. He carried every free state, but not one slave state, and won only 40 percent of the popular vote. Two weeks later, on December 20, South Carolina seceded from the Union, and ten other Southern states followed. The stage was set for the most divisive, painful conflict the country would ever experience.

During the Civil War, Peace Democrats opposed Lincoln and the war, while War Democrats supported both. With the postwar institution of Reconstruction policies created by anti-Southern Radical Republicans, the South became almost completely Democratic—the "solid South" voting block that would endure for more than a century.

The Boy General
The new Brigadier General Custer, shown here in his first photo as a general taken in September 1863. Custer chose a custom-made velvet uniform with flashy gold trim and a crimson tie in order to dazzle and impress his own troops and the enemy's.

Just before they clashed, the Union artillery fired into the mass of gray, staggering them for a moment. Then the Yankee mounted hit. The collision and the close fighting was fearful: Horses went end over end, crushing men beneath them, and sabers and pistols were used point blank. Supported by detachments on either side, the Michiganders turned the gray cavalry. Stuart pulled his troops back.

A Federal force had finally defeated Stuart's feared Invincibles, and in the process saved the Union's victory in the battle that turned the tide of the war. The leader of the triumphant key charge had been Custer, a general for only a week, who had removed all doubt as to his leadership and courage. His men were proud to serve under him—Custer, wrote one, "was not afraid to fight like a private soldier . . . he was ever in front and would never ask them to go where he would not lead." His admiring troops began wearing scarlet neckties,

and before long every man in the brigade wore one as an emblem of honor. Superior officers, too, thought highly of him: Pleasonton privately said that he thought Custer to be the best cavalry general in the world.

Over the next two weeks, the Union cavalry badgered the retreating rebels. On the morning of July 14, Custer's brigade galloped through Williamsburg, Pennsylvania, and drove the remaining graycoats out of town. Then, most of the regiment rode hard downstream toward Falling Waters, Pennsylvania, where a sizable body of Confederates had been sighted. Fighting their way through skirmishers, Custer and an advance squadron stopped at a small wood. Across a field and high on a hill were several earthworks, and behind them were more than two brigades of enemy infantry. The division commander ordered the squadron to charge the hill, and within minutes fifty-seven men under the command of Major Peter Weber ran up

Facing page: **Major General Jeb Stuart**
James Ewell Brown "Jeb" Stuart commanded the Confederate cavalry that confounded the Union army in the first half of the war and inspired Custer's cavalry tactics.

Left: **Battle of Falling Waters**
The Sixth Michigan charges over the rebel earthworks at Falling Waters, Pennsylvania, on July 14, 1863.

Below: **Culpeper Court House**
Custer's cavalry in action at Culpeper Court House, Virginia, on September 14, 1863.

Battle of Brandy Station

In October 1863, at Brandy Station, Virginia, Custer led a charge that broke the Confederate line, but then lost more than 200 men in a hurried Union retreat.

The Bride

Custer and Libbie were married on February 9, 1864, after Custer spent months lobbying Libbie's father, Judge Daniel Bacon, for his permission for them to wed. Here Libbie poses in her wedding dress a few days before their marriage. Custer kept and displayed this photograph for the rest of his life.

the incline. The bluecoats surprised the relaxing rebel army, and soon the squadron was among them. The foremost brigade, more than a thousand stunned men, surrendered. But the second brigade behind them began shooting, and soon many of the prisoners were grabbing their guns and firing away. More than half of the squadron were immediately killed or wounded, and somehow the rest made it back to their lines. The rest of Custer's brigade arrived, and he sent the Sixth Michigan into the melee. He directed the First to the right and the Seventh to the left, then led several charges that won the battle. More than two hours later, those rebels still alive disappeared from the field and across the Potomac. The Michiganders captured several artillery pieces and more than 1,500 prisoners, more than their own number. It was another stunning victory for the Michigan Brigade, and proved that cavalry could be effective even against an entrenched enemy. The Battle of Falling Waters effectively ended the fighting around Gettysburg, and the two armies dug in for the rest of the summer on either side of the Rappahannock.

Skirmishing continued sporadically, and in September, Meade made a weak thrust south of the river. The cavalry was directed to scout in front and guard the infantry's flanks. At Culpeper Court House—Stuart's headquarters—on August 13, the Union cavalry encountered heavy opposition. Custer's horse was hit and killed by an artillery shell as he charged straight toward the heavy guns; the shell nicked his leg, tearing his boot, and bruising the skin badly. He mounted a loose steed as some of his men seized the cannon, then led four regiments down the streets of Culpeper and into the enemy lines. The attack routed the Confederates, who turned and fled. Custer's wound was serious enough to garner him a twenty-day furlough.

Custer arrived in Monroe by train on September 16 to a hero's welcome. His parents were in town, visiting his "second mother"—older sister Lydia—and her family. The entire household greeted him joyously, but the Boy General's top priority was Libbie Bacon, whom he had not seen in five months. Despite her father's continued opposition, he was determined to wed her. Libbie herself had not been consistent in her letters to him, but in truth she had all but succumbed to his advances. Weeks earlier she finally realized that she was in love with him: "There is no similarity of tastes between us," she wrote in her diary, ". . . but I love him." Late in the evening of September 28, after dancing all night at a masquerade party given in his honor, she accepted his proposal. He returned to his command a week later secure in the knowledge that they would marry as soon as it was convenient.

The cavalry spent the next month on raids south behind enemy lines, twice barely escaping with their lives when cut off by superior rebel forces. Near Brandy Station, Custer led the Fifth Michigan in a charge that broke the enemy line and enabled his division to reach the Rappahannock. A few days later, the Union cavalry was led into a trap and mustered a hurried retreat before artillery, infantry, and Stuart's mounted. Custer lost more than 200 men in the two

"There is no similarity of tastes between us . . . but I love him."
—Libbie Bacon, writing of Custer in her diary

Newlyweds
Brigadier General Custer and his new wife Libbie pose at Mathew Brady's studio in February 1864, just days after their wedding.

Brigadier General Hugh Judson Kilpatrick
Kilpatrick graduated from West Point one class ahead of Custer, and rose quickly through the ranks during the war. His troops called him "Kill-Cavalry" due to his disregard for their lives.

actions, an ignoble end to the year's field operations. After the Federals spent a week in late November of halfhearted maneuvering and probing into the Confederate lines, a restless Custer and the rest of Meade's force soon settled down for a long winter, separated from Lee's army by two rivers, the Rappahannock and Rapidan.

By December's end, the Third Cavalry had constructed wooden huts near Brandy Station. The winter was colder than usual, and for the next several months there was little skirmishing between the two armies. It was understood that neither of the picket lines would fire at each other; officers rode along the lines without attracting gunfire. Some of the pickets even traded with their enemy numbers, tobacco for food and the like. The Union cavalry stayed busy with drills and instruction, but life was easier for the officers. A good deal of their time was spent conducting and wagering on horse races, an activity irresistible to Custer.

Aside from judging horseflesh and the routine duties of administering his men, he spent much of his time lobbying with Libbie — and her father — for an early wedding. Under a relentless frontal attack from the cavalryman, Judge Bacon finally relented and gave his blessing. When Libbie agreed to a winter date, Custer was overjoyed. "I am so supremely happy," he wrote her, "that I can scarcely write . . . Am I not dreaming? Surely such unalloyed pleasure never before was enjoyed by mortal man." Libbie was just as blissful: "If loveing with one's whole soul is insanity, I am ripe for an insane asylum." He finally obtained a furlough, and, on January 27, boarded a train for Monroe with three friends from his brigade.

Armstrong and Libbie were married on February 9, 1864, in Monroe's First Presbyterian Church. Custer was in dress uniform and had trimmed his hair for the occasion. Libbie wore a white silk gown with an extensive train. That evening they received 300 guests at the Bacon home. The Boy General impressed many with his devotion to his new bride and his agreeable nature. The Seventh Michigan Cavalry sent them a seven-piece silver tea set, one of many fine wedding gifts. The newlyweds boarded a midnight train for Cleveland, then traveled on to Buffalo and Rochester and the homes of relatives in the area. West Point was next, and New York City and Washington after that. The honeymoon ended when he was ordered by telegram to report for duty immediately. He begged Libbie to stay in the capital, but she refused — she would accompany her husband to his post. A final train ride across the war-ravaged Virginia countryside brought them to brigade headquarters. Libbie was now the wife of a soldier, and her initiation into that life was quick. Until the end, she would be with him whenever possible, and when it was not they would write long, frequent letters overflowing with their love for each other. She would endure the worst hardships of the next twelve years with grace, and would remain happy so long as her Autie was by her side.

Within weeks Custer was back in action. On the last day of February 1864, Custer led a force of four mounted regiments and flying artillery on a secret raid across the Rapidan fifty miles to Charlottesville, Virginia. The action was actually a feint in support of a larger strike centered on Richmond to free the 15,000 Union prisoners there; it was hoped that Lee would swoop down on Custer's brigade allowing the rest of the division to charge into the Confederate capital and capture it. Kilpatrick commanded the force planning to raid Richmond. He was a West Point classmate of Custer's and another "boy general"; he had thundered up the ranks at the expense of plenty of men under him—his men called him "Kill-Cavalry" for his wanton

Raid Across the Rapidan
Custer's men burn the mill at Stanardsville, Virginia, during his raid across the Rapidan River in March 1864.

disregard for their lives. But while Custer's part was judged a success—the brigade made it back by the skin of their teeth, without the loss of a single man—the larger operation failed completely, losing hundreds of men and horses. Kilpatrick attempted a whitewash in his reports, but that didn't take. He was soon reassigned to the Western theater.

A few weeks later the newlyweds used a twenty-day furlough to resume their honeymoon in Baltimore and Washington, where they met President Lincoln and numerous senators and congressmen. Custer was learning how important it was to curry favor with the politically influential. He had risen quickly in the army thanks to perceptive superior officers, but he had seen too many of those superiors removed from command according to the whims of politicians rather than battlefield performances. It was not enough to let one's actions speak for themselves, however glorious they might be.

Custer rejoined his command on April 14, 1864, amid a spring shakeup at the top of the army chain of command that saw the unassuming Ulysses S. Grant made commander-in-chief of all the Federal armies. Grant had overseen a steady string of victories in the Western theater of the war—Shiloh, Vicksburg, and Chattanooga

Major General Wade Hampton

Although he doubted the wisdom of slavery and secession, Hampton led the Confederates at the First Battle of Bull Run, fought at Antietam and Gettysburg, and succeeded Jeb Stuart as cavalry commander of the Army of Northern Virginia. One of the best cavalry leaders of the war, he became famous for his cattle raid, with Brigadier General Thomas L. Rosser, of a Union camp in order to capture nearly 2,500 cattle to feed Confederate troops.

Once over the bridge, the column re-mounted and trotted ahead. The trot became a furious gallop that overwhelmed the enemy force. In a failed counterattack led by Stuart, the rebel general was shot by an unknown Michigander. Within minutes the Union army held the ridge, and the enemy was in full retreat. The Federals had again defeated the Invincibles, whose weaker force could not hold their position—especially considering the coolness under pressure shown by Custer and his Brigade. "Custer's charge . . . was brilliantly executed," wrote Sheridan later. "Beginning at a walk, he increased his gait to a trot, and then at full speed rushed the enemy." Sheridan's opposite number, Stuart, died the next day in Richmond. Yellow Tavern would be remembered as a turning point; never again would the Confederate cavalry dominate the battlefield.

The march toward Richmond resumed. During the night, misled by a bluecoated rebel spy, Custer's division blundered into Richmond's defensive perimeter, and early the next morning came under fire from the city's home guard. When Confederate cavalry attacked the rear of the column, Custer was directed by Sheridan—who by now knew the man to call on when something absolutely had to be done quickly and surely—to take a railroad bridge over the rain-swollen Chickahominy River. Under heavy sniper fire, and without any rest the night before or food or even coffee that morning, his men laid planks over the tracks and he led them on a charge over the river. The charge broke the rebel line, and the Union cavalry followed— though not before two Richmond newsboys (suspected by Sheridan of being spies) strolled boldly among the Union lines selling their newspapers. The corps bivouacked in heavy rain just northeast of the river at Mechanicsville. The next day, they marched east to the James River, then turned north. Sheridan's tired and hungry men rejoined Grant's army on May 24.

The cavalry was ordered south after a few days' rest to help lay a pontoon bridge over the Pamunkey River, where Custer directed the work. The next day, as Federal troops crossed the river, the cavalry clashed with two divisions under Major General Wade Hampton, the late Stuart's best commander and now Sheridan's counterpart, at nearby Haw's Shop. Sheridan ordered Custer's brigade into a wood where the rebels were entrenched. They marched forward on foot, refusing to wilt under a furious fire from musket and artillery, and when the enemy withdrew, they mounted and charged. Horses and men dropped left and right, but the Confederates were routed. The brigade lost forty-one men.

General William Henry Fitzhugh Lee

Lee was the second son of General Robert E. Lee and an excellent cavalry commander in his own right.

Battle of Trevilian Station

James E. Taylor's sketch of the Battle of Trevilian Station in June 1864 shows Brigadier General Thomas L. Rosser (center) waving his hat as he leads his Laurel Brigade against his friend Custer's Wolverines. Custer (right center) reaches to rip his falling guidon from the staff carried by his mortally wounded color bearer, Sergeant Michael Bellior.

After a day and a half of rest, the two armies joined battle again at Cold Harbor, a key position east of Richmond in Grant's drive south. Custer's brigade knocked back an enemy attack with its Spencer carbines on May 30, and on the next day, with rebel artillery shells crashing among them, a First Michigan battalion took Cold Harbor. The Federals dug in and awaited Lee's army, just six miles away. At dawn the next day, the attack came. Inspired by the sight of Custer on horseback along the fieldworks, shouting encouragement to his men, the cavalry held until relieved by infantry at noon. Sheridan's horsemen pulled back and recovered their strength for a week, while some of the bloodiest fighting of the war continued at Cold Harbor—one of Grant's few mistakes. At the week's end, the cavalry was ordered west to take Charlottesville and wreck the Virginia Central Railroad tracks at Trevilian Station and the James River Canal.

At Trevilian Station, Hampton waited with a force roughly equal to Sheridan's 6,000 troopers and three batteries of flying artillery. While part of the two armies engaged on the road to the depot, Custer and his men hit another division and forced them back. He and his advance regiment raced down another road to the railroad tracks, then galloped a mile west to the station, where an artillery battery of Hampton's sat. As the Michiganders stormed into the station, a Confederate regiment attacked from the north led by

> *"Custer's charge . . . was brilliantly executed. Beginning at a walk, he increased his gait to a trot, and then at full speed rushed the enemy."*
> —Major General Phil Sheridan, writing on the Battle of Yellow Tavern

Battle of the Crater

At dawn on July 30, 1864, a huge explosion tore a thirty-foot-deep crater in the ground, creating a gap in the Confederate defenses at Petersburg, Virginia. Unfortunately, Union troops botched the job of actually taking Petersburg: Rather than running around the crater, three divisions ran down into the hole and got stuck there, allowing the Confederates a chance to regroup and shoot straight into them. Rebel troops allowed most of the white Union soldiers to live, but shot and killed all of the black troops.

General Fitzhugh Lee, Custer's former tactics instructor at West Point and the second son of Robert E. Lee. The rest of Custer's brigade arrived in time to repulse them, but within minutes another rebel brigade charged the station from the west, capturing some Federals. A counterattack led by Custer scattered the enemy just as the remainder of Custer's column rode into the station. Custer directed his men to throw down a rail barricade in the road, then had them dismount, load their carbines, and take a breath. In a field devoid of cover, they formed into a circle. They were completely surrounded and outnumbered by two brigades of Stuart's Invincibles: If they could just hold out until the other two cavalry divisions reached them . . . Then the assaults began, lasting over the next several hours. Both sides fought fiercely as the rebels threw everything they had at the Yankees, and the Yankees beat them back at every point on their perimeter. Custer seemed to be everywhere, yelling orders and encouraging his men. Three horses were shot from under him. By the time Sheridan forced a hole through the

The Red Tie Boys

*"With Custer as leader we are all
heroes and hankering for a fight."*
—Third Cavalry Division officer

Throughout the last months of 1864,
the Union army continued to move
south up the Shenandoah Valley into
Virginia. At Fisher's Hill, a wide bluff just
south of Strasburg, twenty miles above
Winchester, the Confederates made
another stand the next day. Early's out-
manned army couldn't hold, though, and
two days later, a cavalry charge on the
western flank and an infantry charge up the
bluff scattered the rebel army. The upper
Shenandoah Valley belonged to the
bluecoats.

Major General Philip H. Sheridan and Staff

*Sheridan's staff in 1864 included men that later
became celebrated Indian fighters—from left,
Generals Sheridan, James Forsyth, Wesley
Merritt, Thomas C. Devin, and Custer.*

Lieutenant General Richard Stoddard "Baldy" Ewell

Ewell was one of the "fightingest" Confederate cavalry commanders Custer ever faced.

A few days later, General James Wilson, commander of the Third Cavalry Division, was transferred to the Western theater to assume command of Sherman's cavalry. Sheridan selected Custer as his new division commander. His men in the Michigan Brigade were shocked. One trooper wrote "i reckon our Brig will go to the divle now, for the want of a commander." Custer told his officers that he would do everything within his power to transfer his Wolverines to the Third Cavalry Division—the Cavalry Corps was set for reorganization after the campaign—but they were distraught. Some cried, others threatened resignation. His new charges were happy at the news and welcomed the change. No doubt visions of glory under their dashing leader danced in their heads.

Custer joined his new troops at Harrisonburg, Virginia, where the Federals had stopped in their pursuit of Early. A few days later, he was directed to torch every house in and around nearby Dayton after a lieutenant who was a favorite of Sheridan's was killed delivering dispatches to Custer. The Third Division burned quite a few houses around the town before Sheridan had a change of heart. Dayton was spared, but the next night the Union forces marched north, and over the next three days the cavalry ranged across the area and razed everything in sight. Chased by the Confederate army, who was ordered by Early to pursue and harass them, it was slow work. "The Burning" was a swath of devastation almost 100 miles in length, and would presage Sherman's similar march through Georgia and the Carolinas.

Their unpleasant work done, the Yankees crossed Tom's Brook near Woodstock on October 8. The rebels camped just south of the creek. Sheridan was enraged by their temerity, and early the next morning two cavalry divisions rode toward the Confederates and reined in along the water. After a lengthy but ineffective artillery exchange, elements of Custer's Third Division tore into the Confederate left flank. Custer led a charge down a road and across Tom's Brook that routed the enemy line. The Union cavalry pursued them relentlessly for more than twenty miles, and captured prisoners, wagons, and supplies. The pell-mell panic was dubbed the "Woodstock Races" by the celebrants. The Third Cavalry Division was jubilant: "With Custer as leader we are all heroes and hankering for a fight," said one of the Third's officers, and soon every man in the division was wearing a scarlet tie. The Red Tie Boys, they now called themselves.

The Union army continued to withdraw, now free from rebel skirmishers. It crossed Cedar Creek and set up camp on its north bank near Middletown. The encampment spread out five miles across the valley, with Custer's Third Division on the western flank. For more than a week the Army of the Shenandoah rested; Sheridan went to Washington for a quick council of war. Then, in the wee hours of October 19, shots rang out along the picket line to the west. Custer awoke and, responding to what was no doubt a small rebel raid, mobilized one regiment and sent them to help defend the line. Within minutes the scattered shots had become a steady roar from the other direction. A breathless messenger told the tale: Early and his ragged army had surprised the infantry on the Union left, and was working his way west. Caught sleeping, the disorganized and demoralized Federals were surrendering by the hundreds, and thousands more were moving down the road toward Winchester, three, four, five divisions and more. Apparently, the small sortie to the west had been a diversion. Despite pockets of resistance here and there, the entire Union army was in danger of being routed.

Custer at Ease
Brigadier General Custer rests at his field headquarters with his Saint Bernard in July 1864.

By daybreak, the Third Division was mounted. Through a thick cover of fog and artillery fire, and past a steady stream of Federal stragglers, the Division swung to the east flank of what was left of the infantry, one division in the fields just north of town. Then Custer and most of his division were ordered into the center of the Federal line, next to Wesley Merritt's cavalry. They checked the enemy advance with their Spencer carbines, and the sight of disciplined horsemen slowed the Confederates. Assuming victory, Early halted his tired and hungry men, many of whom were eating Yankee breakfasts and looting Yankee camps and corpses. Though some of the Union divisions were reforming, there was no serious thought of counterattack. If the Federals could manage an organized retreat, the defeat might be not be so costly.

No sooner had the Yankees turned north about 11 A.M. than they heard a cheer moving toward them from that direction. Riding hard down the valley pike toward them on a foaming horse was Sheridan, waving his cap and rallying his men. He had spent the night in Winchester on his return from the capital and, hearing the roar of battle, jumped on his mount and galloped off. Behind him was a swarm of bluecoats, cheering and brandishing weapons. Little Phil was determined to reorganize the army and fight back right then and there. He rode from group to group, inspiring his half-dressed troops and transforming them into an army again.

When Sheridan reached Custer, the Boy General grabbed his CO in his arms and hugged him. Someone mentioned a retreat, but Sheridan growled, "Retreat—hell! We'll be back in our camps tonight." Then he rode the length of the Union line, his hat in hand, so that every soldier could see him. The cheers were deafening. After assessing the situation, Sheridan moved Custer back to the right flank, and gave him full leeway to "take charge of affairs" there. Custer arrived with his troops and immediately repulsed repeated assaults by the rebel cavalry. At 4 P.M., his army rallied and ready,

Brigadier General Thomas Lafayette Rosser

Rosser was one of Custer's closest friends at West Point, and Custer showed his respect for the Confederate leader by doffing his hat and bowing just before the Battle at Tom's Brook on October 9, 1864.

Sheridan called for a charge. To the blare of bugles and cannon, they attacked. The rebel left flank folded first, then the entire graycoat force was overwhelmed. Custer and his Red Tie Boys galloped south to flood through a hole in the Confederate left. It was the knockout blow. Jubal's army, terrified that their line of retreat was cut off, turned and ran "like a herd of stampeding cattle . . . thousands of rebels indiscriminately mingled together, wearily jogging along . . . hurling away their guns and knapsacks in their fright," as a Union army surgeon observed. The Third Division kept on, through scattered volleys and over stone walls and through the fleeing soldiers, after Early's wagon train. They chased them several miles down the pike, past Strasburg, and gathered a massive amount of booty—forty-five cannon, dozens of vehicles, several flags, a general, and more than a hundred prisoners.

Custer got back to Sheridan's headquarters at a mansion called Belle Grove at 9 P.M. Sheridan walked out to meet him, pulled him from his horse, and said, "You have done it for me this time, Custer!" The Boy General grabbed Sheridan around the waist and hoisted him into the air and giddily whirled him around. He said, "By God, Phil, we've cleaned them out of their guns and got ours back!" An embarrassed Sheridan replied, "There, there, old fellow, don't capture me!" Sheridan telegraphed Grant to recommend a promotion for Custer and two others, and on October 23, 1864, he was officially made a brevet major general.

The Battle of Cedar Creek effectively ended the Shenandoah Valley campaign. Sheridan received acclaim for destroying the

Shenandoah Valley Campaign

On October 7, 1864, in the last days of the Shenandoah Valley campaign, Custer's Third Division burns, destroys, or appropriates everything of value as it covers the withdrawal of the Army of the Shenandoah from the valley. Custer is at lower right.

Sheridan's Ride

Sheridan turned a retreat around and rallied his men to victory at Cedar Creek, Virginia, on October 19, 1864. This painting by T. Buchanan Read celebrated Sheridan's ride.

they lifted and pushed wagons that were sunk up to their hubs. The wagon train halted at dusk six miles short of Dinwiddie Court House. The two armies collided the next afternoon just north of the hamlet, on the road to Five Forks, and the rebels quickly pushed the Yankees south toward town. Sheridan dispatched an aide to Custer. He was to hurry two of his brigades up to Dinwiddie Court House as reinforcements.

Under a new personal guidon crafted from silk by his wife, Custer galloped off with his staff. He arrived at 4 P.M. to find a grim scenario. The two other cavalry divisions, disorganized and undermanned, were barely holding a ragged line just outside the village. Custer rode along the front attempting to rally the troops. Then, when Custer's two brigades caught up, Sheridan dismounted them and stationed them along the road to Five Forks on the Union left facing a huge force of gray infantry. "I want you to *give* it to them," he said to Custer. Then the two armies engaged. The Red Tie Boys moved forward, then were repulsed by fierce rebel fire. The Federals fell back and quickly threw up makeshift rail barricades, then trained their Spencers on Pickett's oncoming troops. They held their fire, then at the last minute let the Southerners have it. The gray line staggered, then fell back in disarray. As darkness came on, Sheridan still held the town. He asked Grant for an infantry corps, and Grant

Battle of Cedar Creek
Sheridan leads his men to victory over Jubal Early's rebels at Cedar Creek, Virginia, on October 19, 1864.

Captured Confederate Colors

On October 23, 1864, Custer presents the thirteen rebel flags captured at the Battle of Cedar Creek to Secretary of War Edwin M. Stanton in Washington, D. C. At the ceremony, Stanton told Custer of his promotion to major general.

sent 12,000 Union infantry under the command of Major General Gouverneur Warren, one of the heroes of Gettysburg. They were set to arrive late that night after a short march. Once they arrived, Sheridan could strike at dawn.

When dawn broke the infantry still hadn't arrived. Pickett, tipped off to the approach of Warren, fell back to Five Forks, five miles away, and erected formidable earthworks. The Union cavalry followed, skirmishing and reconnoitering. Hours of sniping and artillery fire ensued while the furious Sheridan waited for his foot soldiers. They ambled up at 4 P.M., and Sheridan attacked immediately. Custer, on the left, led his Red Ties in a gallop across a large field to outflank the rebels, but a withering fire from musket and artillery met them before they'd gotten halfway across. They fell back and found that the infantry attack on the right had failed. Sheridan rode among the foot soldiers like a man possessed. Finally, he grabbed a battle flag and led them back into the gray line. Custer and his men rode forward again. More than halfway across the field they pitched to the ground before a terrible fusillade. Custer grabbed his fallen guidon, jumped back on his horse, and leaped over the earthworks. His troops followed him in a frenzy, firing their Spencers repeatedly into the enemy. The rebel line fell apart, and Custer turned his men officer to receive personally the Confederate surrender, he rode into the enemy ranks, waving a small white handkerchief over his head. He was directed to Lieutenant General James Longstreet, Lee's second-in-command, where Custer demanded an unconditional surrender. An animated conversation ensued. Longstreet, irritated by the Boy General's temerity, sent him back to his lines, commenting that "General Lee has gone to meet General Grant, and it is for them to determine the future of the armies." When Custer rode through his men with a broad smile on his face, they cheered him. The word spread, and the Yankees began relaxing and celebrating.

Custer made his way to Appomattox Court House that afternoon. At approximately 3 P.M. on April 9, 1865, Lee surrendered to Grant inside the Wilmer McLean farmhouse at Appomattox. Custer waited with other second-rank generals outside. After Lee and Grant left, Sheridan paid McLean twenty dollars for the small oval-topped table upon which Grant had written his generous surrender terms. He presented it to Custer as a gift for Libbie, with a note:

Major General George E. Pickett
Infamous for his disastrous charge at Gettysburg (which was ordered by Robert E. Lee), Pickett commanded the Confederate forces at Five Forks.

> My Dear Madam
> I respectfully present to you the small writing table on which the conditions for the surrender of the Army of Northern Virginia were written by Lt. General Grant—and permit me to say, Madam, that there is scarcely an individual in our service who has contributed more to bring about this desirable result than your gallant husband.
> Very respectfully
> Phil E. Sheridan
> Maj General

Custer spent the rest of the day seeking out and reconciling with Confederate officers, many of them West Point classmates and acquaintances. That night, he labored for a long time over a letter of congratulation to his men. After thanking "the God of battles," and expressing his admiration for his division's heroic record of "indomitable courage . . . unparalleled in the annals of war," he recounted their triumphs. He concluded:

> For our comrades who have fallen, let us ever cherish a grateful remembrance. To the wounded and to those who languish in Southern prisons, let our heartfelt sympathies be tendered.
> And now, speaking for myself alone, when the war is ended and the task of the historian begins; when those deeds of daring which have rendered the name and fame of the Third Cavalry Division imperishable, are inscribed upon the bright pages of our country's history, I only ask that my name be written as that of the commander of the Third Cavalry Division.
> A. Custer
> Brevet Major General

Battle of Five Forks

The Battle of Five Forks, Virginia, on April 1, 1865, was the Waterloo of the Confederacy. Custer and his men captured 4,500 Southerners.

Above: Prisoners of War
Federal troops guard rebel prisoners captured at the Battle of Five Forks on April 1, 1865.

Right: Battle of Sayler's Creek
General "Baldy" Ewell's rebel troops surrender at the Battle of Sayler's Creek, one of the final battles of the war, on April 6, 1865.

Two days later he wrote a short but eloquent letter to Libbie: "My Darling—Only time to write a word. Heart too full for utterance . . . Thank God PEACE is at hand . . ."

Custer garnered lavish praise for his generalship during the Appomattox Campaign. Sheridan recommended a promotion to brevet major general in the regular army for his "personal gallantry and high ability" over the previous month's action, and that was soon confirmed.

Armstrong united with Libbie a week later. She found her husband haggard and drawn. As he wrote to his sister, "I never needed rest so much as I do now."

Flag of Truce
Custer receives the flag of surrender from Confederate Captain R. M. Sims on April 9, 1865. The makeshift flag was a white towel with a red border.

Surrender at Appomattox
This engraving of a sketch by A. R. Waud shows Robert E. Lee signing the terms of surrender inside the Wilmer McLean farmhouse at Appomattox, Virginia, on April 9, 1865. Grant wrote out the terms on a separate table, which was bought by Sheridan and given to Libbie Custer.

On Tuesday, May 23, the Army of the Potomac paraded down Pennsylvania Avenue past the White House. Custer rode at the head of his Third Division near the forefront of the Grand Review. The crowd ogled and cheered the cavalry commander who'd had twelve horses shot from under him, and many of them garlanded his thoroughbred mount, Don Juan, with wreaths of flowers. As he neared the reviewing stand, Custer's steed, a former racehorse, bolted past the President and other dignitaries. His hat and saber fell to the ground as Custer reined his mount in to cheers from the crowd. Some thought the timing a bit too convenient—or was it just more of Custer's Luck?

CUSTERS OF THE SOUTH

During his battles in Virginia and Pennsylvania, the Boy General fought against several courageous Confederate cavalry commanders, a few of whom were personal friends. Like Custer, these men proved themselves in battle.

Thomas Lafayette Rosser, a tall, handsome, Virginia-born Texan, had been a classmate and close friend of Custer's at West Point. At the outset of the conflict he was only a second lieutenant, but by September 1863 he had risen to brigadier general. He was an audacious, never-say-die cavalry commander and a continual thorn in Sheridan's side during the Shenandoah campaign of 1864. He was particularly adept at bold raids behind the Union lines.

Fitzhugh Lee, the easygoing second son of Robert E. Lee, had been Custer's instructor of tactics at West Point. He also entered the war a lieutenant and quickly rose through the ranks to become a major general by August 1863. Despite mutterings of nepotism, he proved himself a hard fighter and resourceful commander, distinguishing himself at Yellow Tavern and Trevilian Station. He could cover the rear of a retreating army like no other, a dubious distinction that came in handy in the war's latter stages. During the Appomattox Campaign, he commanded the Army of Northern Virginia's cavalry, and for almost a solid month guarded his father's rear on the final retreat to Appomattox.

Wade Hampton was reputedly the richest planter in the South. He had no military training or experience, and harbored doubts about the economic benefits of slavery. But when war broke out, the strapping South Carolinian raised a regiment of 1,000 men—Hampton's Legion—and installed himself as commanding colonel. Hampton was fiercely intelligent and a born soldier, and he soon proved his mettle in battle. By May 1862 he was a brigadier general, and by that September he was second in command to Jeb Stuart. After Stuart was mortally wounded at Yellow Tavern in May 1864, Hampton assumed command of Lee's cavalry.

There had been some hesitation about putting him in charge, but several victories—including his famous raid on Grant's herd of 2,500 cattle in September 1864—put to rest any fears about his competence.

The man most similar to Custer was James Ewell Brown "Jeb" Stuart. Like Custer, Stuart had a reputation for occasional recklessness, impressive physical endurance, and supreme courageousness. He was also a bit of a dandy—his short jacket, gold braid, ostrich plume, high black boots, jangling golden spurs, and well-groomed whiskers garnered him the nickname "Beauty," and his outsized ego demanded fulsome praise. But he was an outstanding tactician and inspiring leader who fought brilliantly in many major battles and always where the action was thickest. He was Robert E. Lee's eyes and ears, especially during the early years of the war, and his bold raids against Yankee communications and supply centers and trains gathered information that helped thwart several Union campaigns. Twice he rode completely around McClellan's Army of the Potomac, once in June 1862 and again in October 1862. Though he was criticized for his actions at Gettysburg—he took off on a raid that kept him out of touch for more than ten days, and only arrived on the battlefield on the second day, leading some to place much of the blame for the Confederate defeat at his feet—his death in May 1864 at Yellow Tavern at the hands of Custer's Michigan Brigade was a huge loss to the Confederate cause.

Still, had Stuart survived, he would have made little difference to the war's outcome. By 1864, it was too late: His men were outnumbered, poorly mounted, and under-supplied. Many rebel troopers wore uniform parts of blue, plundered from the Union dead, and the Union cavalry's Spencer repeating rifle made a big difference in close action. The Confederate cavalry was hungry, exhausted, and demoralized, and clearheaded observers knew it was just a matter of time and attrition. No amount of bold cavaliers would change the course of the war.

Cavalry Skirmish

Until Hooker reorganized the Union cavalry, Jeb Stuart's cavalry—shown here in an 1862 skirmish—ran rings (literally) around the Army of the Potomac.

The man most similar to Custer was James Ewell Brown "Jeb" Stuart. Like Custer, Stuart had a reputation for occasional recklessness, impressive physical endurance, and supreme courageousness. He was also a bit of a dandy— his short jacket, gold braid, ostrich plume, high black boots, jangling golden spurs, and well-groomed whiskers garnered him the nickname "Beauty," —his outsized ego demanded fulsome praise.

Chapter 4

The Seventh Cavalry

"He [Custer] appears to be mad about something, and is very much on his dignity."
—Captain Albert Barnitz, Seventh Cavalry

Like many young men who came of age participating in war, Custer found peace unsettling. When a man has spent a significant part of his formative years under combat conditions, the heart-pumping knowledge that any second may be your last does curious things to him. Some break. Others adapt for a while, and bear the intense pressures that hone a man's senses to a razor-sharp pitch. But there are certain men who thrive on that edge, who are energized by, and become accustomed to,

The Great Buffalo Hunt
Custer set forth to the American West in 1865, where the U.S. Army was battling the Indians as part of the nation's war for Manifest Destiny. This oil painting was created by William Robinson Leigh in 1947.

that constant danger. Those are the born warriors. Custer was one of those. He loved war, and the glory and adulation that war brought him.

Adjusting to the pace of peace was difficult for Custer. A spell of R&R was one thing—those twenty-day furloughs were bearable as he got to see his true love, and besides, it was only for a while. But permanent peace was another thing entirely; not to feel that preciousness of life that can only be fully known when one is close to death, not to know the transcendent glory of leading men you loved, and who loved you, into battle—well. Custer didn't know about that. Besides, he missed seeing his name in the papers.

So he was a happy man in late May 1865 when a message from Sheridan was delivered to him marked "Confidential." Grant had sent Little Phil to New Orleans to assemble an army and march to Texas to hunt down the last of the unrepentant rebel forces. That was the official reason. The unofficial reason was that the Federal army might also mobilize against Emperor Ferdinand Maximilian, the French puppet across the Rio Grande in Mexico. Thousands of French troops occupied Mexico City, and now that the Civil War was over, upholding the Monroe Doctrine—and eliminating the budding French empire in the New World— became a top priority.

Sheridan requested Custer and Wesley Merritt as his cavalry commanders. Custer was to organize a mounted division of 4,000 men at Alexandria, Louisiana, and march to Texas. An excited Custer, his staff, and his Libbie journeyed west by train, then steamboated down to New Orleans where he reported to Sheridan. The last Confederates had surrendered. Sheridan would now deploy more than 30,000 troops along the Mexican border and prepare for action.

After a week of shopping and entertainment in the Crescent City, Custer's party took another steamboat up the Red River to Alexandria. They arrived there in late June 1865, and the Custers settled into a large deserted plantation house. The five regiments arrived over the next two weeks. Then, Custer ran into problems he never had to worry about during the war.

For the first time, Custer ran into hostility and resentment that he couldn't overcome with an inspiring saber charge into the thick of the enemy. His troopers were veteran volunteers, not regular soldiers, and many had fought the Confed-

Moving West
Custer and Libbie pose on their horses at Hempstead, Texas, on October 18, 1865.

Texas Headquarters
Custer's headquarters at the asylum for the blind in Austin, Texas, November 1865.

That's where the 55,000-man postwar U.S. Army came in. The army would be slashed in half by 1874, but it was spread over a vast expanse between the Mississippi and the Rockies and from Canada to Mexico to fight in the cause of Manifest Destiny.

Tensions between the white settlers and the Indians increased during the Civil War. Soldiers and officers accustomed to dealing and fighting with Indians were shipped east to battle the Confederates, and undisciplined volunteer units replaced them. Indians responded to incursions into their land by increasing raids and atrocities, many of them centered on the railroad lines and their construction crews; they knew what the completion of the railways would mean to their way of life. When the white man killed an Indian it was viewed as Manifest Destiny, but if an Indian killed a white it was an atrocity. The Indians' depredations resulted in the massacre and mutilation of more than 100 peace-seeking Southern Cheyenne women and children at Sand Creek in Colorado Territory by a contingent of volunteer Colorado cavalry under the command of the maniacal Colonel John M. Chivington in November 1864. Though a faction of the weary Cheyenne agreed to a treaty of peace that essentially handed over all of the Colorado Territory soon after, the Sand Creek Massacre further hardened the resolve of most of the hostile Indians on the Northern Plains, and put an end to the idea that they would leave their ancestral lands without a fight.

A network of more than 100 forts, most of them hastily constructed and badly designed, was built along the frontier to protect the railroads, the settlers, and their settlements as they spread into Indian country. Then the army—usually the cavalry, given the immenseness of the Great Plains—was directed to pursue the raiding Indians, whose grass-fed ponies were faster than the heavier, grain-fed cavalry mounts. The Indians mastered the art of guerrilla warfare, and the speed with which they struck and then disappeared into thin air without a trail made them almost impossible to find. Hampered by their need to stick close to their slow-moving supply wagons, the cavalry columns rarely caught their quarry. A cavalryman spent most of his time in the saddle in pursuit of an enemy he never saw, muttering loudly about cowardly Indians who wouldn't stand and fight.

By the time Custer returned to Fort Riley in December 1866, only three companies of the Seventh were still there. The rest had been assigned to garrison other one- or two-company forts to the west. This was standard practice, as a regiment's full complement rarely came together save for large-scale campaigns.

That same month, near Fort Phil Kearny in Wyoming Territory, Captain William J. Fetterman and his eighty-one-man squadron were lured into a trap and slaughtered by Red Cloud's Oglala Lakota. The cocky Fetterman ignored his CO's warnings and strayed

Captain William Fetterman
The brash and overconfident Fetterman had nothing but contempt for the Indian style of fighting. In 1866, he led eighty-one men in pursuit of fleeing Indians along the Bozeman Trail near Fort Phil Kearny, Nebraska Territory. It was a trap. Soon he and his men were surrounded by 2,000 warriors and slaughtered to the last man.

The Hancock Expedition

Hancock's expedition served as Custer's Indian-fighting baptism. Here, the troops bivouac at Fort Harker, Kansas, in April 1867.

Major General Winfield Scott Hancock

A superb Civil War leader, Hancock had no talent for Indian negotiations. His arrogant and disrespectful attitude and harsh tactics only exacerbated the violence on the frontier.

too far from the fort while escorting a wood-bearing train. It was the worst defeat the army had suffered in Plains Indian warfare. To discourage the Indians from further warfare, or to finally lick them, a show of force was decided upon.

Late in March 1867, Major General Winfield Scott Hancock, commander of the Department of the Missouri, led 1,400 infantry, cavalry, and artillery from his forts, down the Santa Fe Trail to the Arkansas River. Commanding the cavalry was Custer, at the head of eleven companies of the Seventh Cavalry. When the column reached Fort Larned, Kansas, on Pawnee Fork, Hancock sent for the Indian leaders. On April 12, twelve Southern Cheyenne and Lakota chiefs rode into camp to parley—Custer's first meeting with hostile Indians.

Hancock was an excellent Civil War general, but he was the worst kind of Indian negotiator. His intentional lack of respect, bellicose posturing, and threats only heightened tensions and made a peaceful conclusion doubtful. So when the wary Indians balked and left for their camp thirty miles away, Hancock decided to march to their village and camp nearby. Directed to meet the next morning, the frightened Indians—with Sand Creek still fresh in their minds— fled in the night. Hancock sent the cavalry in pursuit the next day, and Custer soon learned how different—and difficult—chasing Indians would be. The Indians headed northwest, and soon split into small bands. The Seventh pushed forward, following the dwindling trail. Three days from Larned they reached a stage line known as Smoky Hill Road, and for miles along it Custer found burning houses and stage depots and the charred and mutilated bodies of white settlers.

While pursuing the Indians, Custer spied a buffalo on the horizon. The hunter in him couldn't resist—he had never shot one before—and he spurred Custis Lee, Libbie's favorite mount, in pursuit. Only his dogs followed, and the chase took him out of sight of the column. Bearing down upon the bison, Custer pulled the trigger of his pistol, but the buffalo turned suddenly. Custis Lee threw his head up and the slug plowed into him, killing him instantly and throwing Custer. The buffalo stopped and faced him, then trotted away. His column found him and his dogs hours later. It was a story that Custer would relish telling on himself later.

When Hancock heard of the atrocities against the stations along Smoky Hill Road, he burned the abandoned Indian village near Fort Larned, though the reason for the Indians' flight was clear even to Custer: "The stampede of the Indians from the village, I attributed entirely to fear," he wrote to Libbie a few weeks later. The chase was futile. The Seventh found no Indians, not even a trail to follow. An entire Indian camp, women and children included, had given them the slip. Custer would spend a good part of the summer looking for Indians with little luck. It was an ignominious beginning to his Indian-fighting career.

The regiment trudged into Fort Hays, Kansas, to stock up—only to find that their expected supplies had been delayed. They twiddled their thumbs for several weeks. The inaction, and the time away from Libbie (despite a two-week visit from her), almost drove Custer mad. He took it out on his men, and as he had during his Reconstruction duty, imposed to-the-letter discipline that was harsh and unreasonable. Custer shaved several troopers' heads after they left the post for less than an hour to purchase tinned peaches to fight off scurvy as they were provided no fruits or vegetables. Captain Albert Barnitz, an officer who had served with

Razing Tepees
After the Cheyenne and Lakota evaded Hancock's negotiating party in April 1867, the Federal troops burned the Indian village at Pawnee Fork.

Scouts
The Hancock Expedition was led by a group of scouts, including, from left, chief of scouts Will Comstock, half-Cheyenne scout Ed Guerrier, courier Thomas Atkins, and a young courier named Kincade.

him during the Civil War and admired him greatly, was sorely disappointed in this Custer, calling him an "incarnate fiend" in a letter to his wife. He went on to say, "He appears to be mad about something, and is very much on his dignity." Theodore Davis, a correspondent for *Harper's Weekly* who visited Fort Hays then, also noted Custer's bad humor, describing him as "depressed" and "moody."

On June 1, 1867, Custer and six companies rode out on another fruitless sweep north through hostile Indian territory, south of the Platte River and along the Republican. Nine days later, they reached Fort McPherson on the Platte in Nebraska, where Custer met with Pawnee Killer and other Lakota chiefs and was assured of their peaceful intentions. An angry General Sherman, who arrived at the fort the next day, sent the Seventh out after the Lakota again, this time west toward Fort Sedgwick, Colorado. Indian promises were worthless, Sherman told Custer. Sherman promised that he would arrange for Libbie to join her husband by rail, since it looked as if Custer might be needed in the area through the fall. The six companies left for Sedgwick on June 17.

From that date onward it seemed that Custer's decisions were based less on his orders and the safety of his men than on his desire to reunite with Libbie. Four days later, a bit more than halfway to Sedgwick, he changed his plans. From a camp on the Republican he sent a company of men south to Fort Wallace, Kansas, for supplies instead of to Sedgwick—the chance that Libbie might be there was most likely the true reason—and another company in the same direction to Beaver Creek. Two days later, what remained of the regiment skirmished with a force of Lakota and again parleyed with Pawnee Killer. Their presence persuaded Custer to send another company to find the company at Beaver Creek and escort the supply wagon train from Wallace. His instincts were correct: When the squadron found the wagons two days later, they chased off 200 attacking Indians. The entire contingent reached Custer the next day. Libbie had not been at Wallace. Where was she?

Custer pushed his regiment west, becoming increasingly worried about his wife. They

James Butler "Wild Bill" Hickok

Hickock wore many hats in the American West, from gunfighter to U.S. marshal, Union army spy to actor. He also scouted for Custer during the Hancock Expedition of 1867.

Standoff

Custer enjoyed telling the tale of how he faced a buffalo in a standoff after he accidentally shot his horse while hunting on his own in 1867. This sketch by Western realist artist Frederic Remington depicted the event.

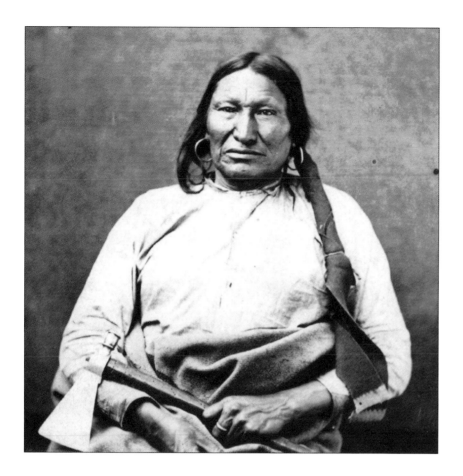

Pawnee Killer
The Oglala chief led Custer on a wild chase during the summer of 1867.

reached Riverside Station, just west of Fort Sedgwick, on July 5 after a grueling march. That night thirty troopers deserted. Orders wired from Sedgwick directed the Seventh south to Fort Wallace, along the Smoky Hill Road. Indians had attacked again, and Custer's men were needed. His men were exhausted and his supplies were low, but he broke camp the next day. When thirteen men deserted during a noon stop, Custer sent Major Joel Elliott, a gung-ho young officer, and some men to "bring back none of those men alive." By the time they returned, two deserters had been wounded and another killed when they opened fire on Elliott's party. Custer loudly denied the column's surgeon permission to treat them, although in private he told him to proceed. A week later they arrived at Fort Wallace.

At Wallace, Custer lost all reason. All he could think about was the danger Libbie might be in. With three officers and seventy-two men riding behind him on the regiment's best mounts, he headed east on the Smoky Hill Road on July 15.

Later, Custer would list several reasons for the ride—the need for supplies, fresh horses, new orders, and cholera medicine—but none stood up under scrutiny. Along the way, he stopped a mail stage and searched through it for letters from Libbie. Further along, a deserter rode off. Custer ordered a sergeant and six men in pursuit. They captured the trooper, but were attacked by hostiles on the way back, and left one man killed and another wounded. His men and

Buffalo: The "Staff of Life"

It is doubtful that any one animal ever dominated the existence and culture of a human race more than the buffalo did the Plains Indian. Before extensive contact with the white man, most of what the Plains Indians used or owned was derived from the buffalo. Many of them scorned those tribes that engaged in farming or cattle herding, so they had to maximize those resources they encountered in their wanderings. Their nomadic existence revolved in large part around the buffalo, as bands and villages followed the large roaming herds all over the Great Plains for most of the year. One Indian agent called it the "staff of life" to the Plains tribes.

The Indians derived more than eighty products from the buffalo. They ate the meat, marrow, tongue, liver, intestines and other innards, and preserved the marrow and meat as jerky. From the hide they made any number of items, including all manner of clothing, tepee covers, bedding, bags, shields, drums, saddles, and dolls. They used the horns and bones, the hair, hooves, tail, sinew, bladder, stomach, and brain—even the chips were burned for fuel and used for ceremonial smoking.

The animal also figured prominently in Plains Indian ceremony and religion. The buffalo was considered the wisest and most powerful of creatures, and closest to the higher powers in Indian religion. The rare white buffalo was the most revered, and a white buffalo robe was worn only by the most distinguished tribal leaders. Some tribes, including the Lakota, wore buffalo-horn headresses and bonnets, which were reserved for high-ranking warriors and were believed to give protection in battle.

Buffalo-Skull Ceremony

The buffalo played an important role in Plains Indian religion and ceremonies. Here, Oglala Lakota place a painted buffalo skull on a bed of sage in a Hunka ceremony, which expressed a father's blessings for his child.

Serious depletion of the buffalo herds began in the mid-nineteenth century. White settlements spread over the buffalo's range, and increasing demand for buffalo hides brought thousands of commercial hunters. In the mid-1870s, buffalo were being slaughtered at a rate of more than one million a year, and soon the self-sufficiency of the Plains Indians was compromised. They became more dependent on U.S. government rations at the agencies. Some tribes, such as those belonging to Sitting Bull and Crazy Horse, refused to submit to this forced obedience. The Sioux War of 1876 was the result.

Last of the Buffalo

American painter Albert Bierstadt was famous for his romantic vision of North America's grandeur, and this 1889 oil painting of an Indian spearing a gigantic buffalo bull was part of his mythologizing of the West.

Bonefields

After the white buffalo hunters had done their work, the remains of the great buffalo herds were spread over the prairies. Some westward-bound pioneers reported that the prairies were so white with bones they looked as if they were covered by snow.

It is doubtful that any one animal ever dominated the existence and culture of a human race more than the buffalo did the Plains Indian.

Indian Fighter

*"There is, perhaps, no other officer of equal
rank [than Custer] on this line who has
worked more faithfully against the Indians,
or who has acquired the same degree of
knowledge of the country and
of the Indian character."*
—Colonel Samuel D. Sturgis

Ten months later, in Monroe, Custer once more received a missive from his friend Phil Sheridan:

Headquarters Department of the Missouri
in the Field, Fort Hays, Kansas
September 24, 1868
General G. A. Custer, Monroe, Michigan:
  Generals Sherman, Sully, and myself, and nearly all the officers of your regiment, have asked for you, and I hope the application will be successful. Can you come at

Battle of the Washita

*Custer's destruction of Black Kettle's sleeping
village of Cheyennes at dawn on November 27,
1868, made the Civil War hero into a celebrated
Indian fighter. Though the Battle of the Washita
was derided by critics in the East as a cold-
blooded massacre, it became a formula for
success in the Indian wars.*

once? Eleven companies of your regiment will move about the 1st of October against the hostile Indians, from Medicine Lodge creek toward the Wichita mountains.

(*Signed*) P. H. Sheridan, Major General Commanding

The Custers had spent the winter and spring in Sheridan's empty quarters at Fort Leavenworth, where they enjoyed a busy social season, and Custer began to write installments of a memoir. In June, they had returned to the Bacon mansion in Monroe. The telegram from Sheridan found Custer restless and ready for action, exactly what Sheridan had hoped for.

In the fourteen months since Custer's arrest, relations with the Indians had gone from bad to worse—particularly on the Northern Plains, where the railroads were inching through Indian hunting grounds. Congress, impatient with the army's lack of progress and pressured by a burgeoning peace movement in the East, had appointed a peace commission to negotiate with the Indians, and in October 1867, the commission met with chiefs of several Indian tribes at Medicine Lodge, Kansas. They had persuaded the Indians to sign away their hunting grounds between the Platte and Arkansas Rivers and take their people to reservations in Indian Territory. In return, the Indians would receive annuities for thirty years. In spring 1868, at Fort Laramie, Wyoming, the commission managed to obtain the signatures of a few minor Lakota chiefs to a treaty, but it was not until November that the indomitable Lakota war chief Red Cloud finally agreed to move to a huge reservation that consisted of most of what would become the state of South Dakota west of the Missouri. The treaty also provided the Lakota with hunting rights north of the Platte. The Powder River country was designated "unceded Indian territory": No whites would be allowed there unless three-fourths of the adult male Lakota voted to permit it.

The "unceded territory" proved to be a problem for it was there that thousands of "nontreaty" Indians roamed at will, following war chiefs such as Gall, Crow King, Lame Deer, Crazy Horse, and the medicine chief Sitting Bull. These chiefs had not signed the treaties,

Mule Race Broadside

Custer, although tireless when on a campaign or in battle, often grew bored during periods of inactivity. At Fort Leavenworth, Kansas, in June 1868, he and his officers passed the time with diversions such as this mule race.

Fort Laramie Treaty Negotiations

In 1868, U.S. commissioners, including General William S. Harney (with the white beard) and General Sherman (to the right of Harney) meet with Lakota and Arapaho Indians to negotiate the Fort Laramie Treaty.

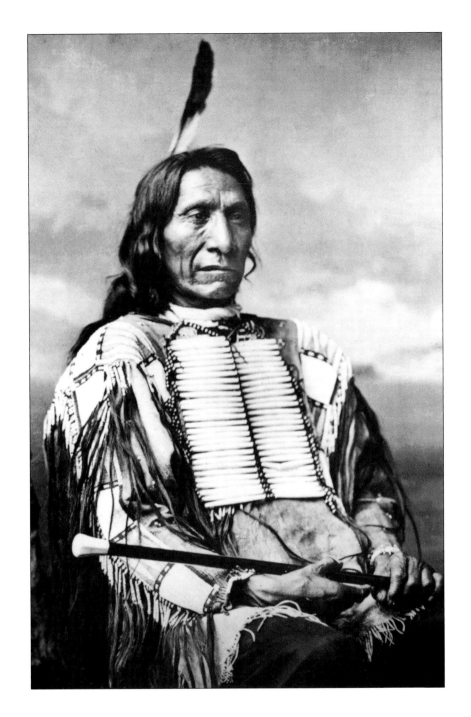

Red Cloud

The Oglala Lakota chief Red Cloud was the only Plains Indian to win a war against the white man. Only when his demanding terms were met would he sign the 1868 Fort Laramie Treaty.

Lakota Chiefs

Lakota chiefs at Fort Laramie in 1868, on hand to forge a treaty, included from left, Spotted Tail, Roman Nose, Old Man Afraid of His Horses, Lone Horn, Whistling Elks, Pipe, and an unidentified chief.

Bivouac
Custer, in a white hat looking towards the right, sits with his men at Camp Forsyth on the Arkansas River in October 1868, just prior to the Washita Campaign.

The Indians at Medicine Lodge had no real idea of what they actually agreed to, and the treaties proved to be difficult to uphold. In July 1868, after nine months of relative peace, full-scale hostilities erupted.

and they looked askance at any attempts by white men to seize or colonize their traditional hunting grounds. They were a constant, serious impediment to "progress," and their free life attracted reservation Indians during the warm summer months. Ironically, the Lakota were an expansionist people themselves; for at least two centuries they were forced westward by other tribes and the whites, and they crushed smaller tribes on their way.

The Indians at Medicine Lodge had no real idea of what they actually agreed to, and the treaties proved to be difficult to uphold. In July 1868, after nine months of relative peace, full-scale hostilities erupted. Sheridan sent out sorties to strike at the hostiles, but they failed, largely due to the ineffectiveness of his field commanders. Hence, his telegram to Custer.

What little, if any, contrition Custer had mustered now dissolved. The army needed him, Custer, the Boy General, to beat the Indians where nobody else could. Sheridan also asked Washington to remit the remainder of Custer's sentence. Custer packed a bag, kissed Libbie goodbye, and left Monroe by the next train, accompanied only by three of his dogs.

By the time he reached Fort Hays, a layer of snow had fallen on the Great Plains. Army campaigns traditionally ended at winter's onset and only resumed after the spring thaw. The Indians knew this, so in the spring they holed up in hard-to-reach camps. Sheridan told Custer that he wanted to try something new—a winter campaign. Hit the Indian villages when they least expected it, when their ponies were weak and their supplies low. True, both Indians and scouts thought that white men could not survive the blizzards. Even the legendary mountain man, Jim Bridger, counseled Sheridan against it. But Little Phil and Custer, eager to prove his mettle again, were convinced that it could be done.

Custer wasted no time. His regiment was encamped on Cavalry Creek, forty miles south of Fort Dodge, Kansas. He rode down to camp and immediately sent out three columns in search of Indians.

Battle of the Washita
This woodcut of James E. Taylor's sketch shows Custer's massacre of Black Kettle's peaceful village on the Washita River in 1868.

Then, as the Cheyennes slept, he quietly deployed four battalions around the encampment of fifty-one lodges. They would attack simultaneously from the northeast, south, west, and north, where Custer would signal the charge with music from the band.

At the first sign of dawn, an Indian, likely Black Kettle, stepped out of his tepee, saw the mounted bluecoats on the other side of the stream, and fired a single rifle shot heavenward in alert. The shivering cavalry band struck up an Irish barroom tune called "Garryowen," and the Seventh Cavalry attacked.

Or at least part of it did. The two southernmost battalions were nowhere to be seen, but the other two splashed across the icy stream and swooped down upon the camp. Captain Albert Barnitz remembered: "We heard the band on the ridge beyond [the ravine] strike up the familiar tune . . . and the answering cheers of the men, as Custer, and his legion came thundering down the long divide . . . the Indian village rang with unearthly war-whoops, the quick discharge of fire-arms, the clamorous barking of dogs, the cries of infants and the wailing of women." The sleeping village erupted as warriors, women, and children dashed from their tepees. Troopers galloped among them, shooting, slashing, and running down the enemy. The two columns from the south rode in late and too far west, and many

Major Joel H. Elliott
Elliott and nineteen of his men were left for dead by Custer at the Battle of the Washita. Benteen's subsequent anonymous letter to the press about Elliott's death intensified the rift in the Seventh Cavalry's officer corps.

Indian Prisoners

Custer and his men captured fifty-three women and children at the Battle of the Washita. This group of Indian prisoners was photographed at Camp Supply.

Kiowa chief Satanta

Kiowa chief Lone Wolf

Indians ran around their flank and escaped. Black Kettle and his wife were shot at the river and fell into the water dead. Others ran into the waters and waded downstream.

In ten minutes, the battle was over, save for isolated pockets of Indians trying to fight their way free. Custer told an officer to stop his men from firing into a group of women and children and take them prisoners. There were few white casualties—only one death and a dozen or so wounded. Captain Hamilton, so young and promising, had been shot through the heart and died in the first charge, and Barnitz was seriously injured. Custer's company commanders estimated 103 Indian braves dead, though probably no more than 38 were warriors. The majority were probably women and children—some innocent, some fighting for their lives alongside the warriors. Fifty-two prisoners were taken, all of them women, children, and old men, and they were given horses to ride.

Lieutenant Edward Settle Godfrey led a platoon of men south of the village and down the valley gathering up ponies. He returned with grim news: He had seen hundreds of tepees downstream and many warriors headed their way, no doubt alerted by the gunfire. Black Kettle's village was only one of several larger winter camps of Arapaho, Kiowa, Cheyenne, and Comanche, and hundreds, perhaps thousands, of fighting men were swarming toward the regiment.

Custer set out a skirmish line to hold off the Indians, who didn't seem intent on a full-scale attack at the moment. Then he put into practice the precepts of total war as laid out by Sheridan and Sherman: total destruction of anything of use to the enemy. His men set fire to everything in the village. Then they shot or slashed the throats of almost 900 Indian ponies. As the troopers fed the bonfires through the afternoon, they uncovered ample evidence—photograph albums, mail, pieces of bedding, and other household items—that young men of the village had indeed raided into Kansas. Little

Rock's twenty-year-old sister Mo-nah-see-tah, a captive, corroborated that fact. The attractive Mo-nah-see-tah traveled with Custer as a negotiator (though she spoke no English) through the rest of the winter. She also, it seems likely, shared his bed until she was released in the spring.

Custer's position was becoming more difficult by the minute, and might turn untenable. The pressure from the warriors moving upstream was mounting. The supply train, protected by a small force of soldiers, was nowhere to be seen and in danger of discovery, at least so Custer thought. And the men's overcoats and haversacks, which they had doffed before attacking, had been seized by the Indians.

Another problem presented itself. That morning, the ambitious Major Elliott had galloped off with a detachment of nineteen men after a group of fleeing Indians, shouting, "Here goes for a brevet or a coffin!" While downstream, Godfrey had heard heavy carbine fire across the river and thought Elliott may have run into fierce opposition. Custer sent Captain Edward Myers down the valley to look for Elliott, but he returned without success. The enemy forces were increasing. Military custom dictated that a commander—especially a victorious one—never leave a battlefield while men were still unaccounted for. But they were gone, probably dead, and their fate was balanced by the safety of the regiment. Custer ordered the regiment to mount, then marched his men and their captives downstream toward the Indian camps in a show of strength. When the warriors ran back to protect their families, Custer turned the column around and quickly left the valley under cover of darkness. They marched through the night with only a few hours' rest, and reached their supply wagons by midmorning.

The Seventh arrived at Camp Supply on December 2. Company by company, and led by a slender rider in fringed buckskin who looked more like a scout than a regimental commander, they paraded smartly before an elated Sheridan and his staff to "Garryowen"—now and forever the regiment's signature song—and saluted him with their sabers. Custer and his men had forged a dramatic victory that crippled the Cheyennes and demoralized the other tribes, and gave the military the decisive victory it so badly needed.

Five days later, Sheridan and Custer led the column out again, marching south toward the remaining hostile bands. On the Washita, two miles from the charred remains of Black Kettle's camp, they found the mutilated remains of Elliott and his men, who had apparently been surrounded and overwhelmed. The campsites downstream were deserted. Sheridan wanted the remaining renegades in the area rounded up and herded onto reservations, and he

Custer in Buckskins

Fresh from the Washita Campaign, Custer poses in his buckskin hunting outfit and burly beard at Fort Sill in the Wichita Mountains in Indian Territory on February 9, 1869.

Colonel Nelson A. Miles
A long-lasting friendship between Miles and the Custers began when they all lived at Big Creek near Fort Hays, Kansas, in the summers of 1869 and 1870.

Colonel Samuel D. Sturgis
Sturgis assumed official command of the Seventh Cavalry in June 1869, but Custer led the regiment in the field while Sturgis pushed papers on detached duty.

ordered Custer after them. They followed a trail down the Washita toward Fort Cobb, 100 miles downriver. Near the fort they skirmished with a band of Kiowas, then camped.

Soon the dangers of a winter campaign caught up with Custer. Rations were low, supply trains were late, and there wasn't enough forage for the horses and mules, who died in droves—the snow, mud, and cold were hard enough on the men, but for the animals it was murder. Despite these obstacles, Custer spent the rest of the winter marching around the Wichita Mountains, rounding up friendlies and running down hostile Cheyenne. The highlight of the campaign was his dramatic and dangerous rescue of two white women from a Cheyenne camp—where he also displayed skill in preventing the revenge-minded regiment of Kansas volunteers from annihilating the village. But other Cheyenne and Kiowa bands known to have white captives eluded him, and more than once his starving men were forced to eat horsemeat.

On March 28, 1869, the expedition limped into Camp Supply, finished. The campaign had started with a bang, but it ended with mixed results. Though the Washita area was finally free of hostiles, there were still plenty of nonreservation Indians roaming the Plains. The Cheyenne would ultimately be subdued, but not by Custer: On July 11, 1869, Major Eugene A. Carr's Fifth Cavalry would defeat them decisively at Summit Springs, Colorado. The remaining Cheyenne were soon settled on their new reservation near Camp Supply.

The Battle of the Washita proved to be a blueprint for success, one repeated over and over across the western plains until the free-roaming Indians were hounded into submission. And though derided by some army critics in the East as a cold-blooded slaughter, a massacre inflicted upon a friendly village, the Washita put Custer back on the front page and in a new role. The Civil War hero was now a successful Indian fighter.

The fate of Major Elliott and his nineteen men, however, would intensify the factions within the regiment, especially within the officer corps. Few of them criticized Custer in the heat of battle—and while facing a large force of hostiles gathering nearby and likely preparing to attack—for his decision to leave the Washita with twenty of his men unaccounted for, though only a cursory search had been made. But while most of the cavalrymen had agreed with Custer that Elliott had probably been overwhelmed by a superior enemy force, the subject refused to die. Two months later, the *St. Louis Democrat* printed an anonymous letter from a participant in the battle that accused Custer of callously abandoning his men. In an emotionally charged meeting with his officers, Custer swore he would horsewhip the letter-writer. Captain Benteen, who had hated Custer since their first meeting (and was chaffed that his exploits at the Washita had gone unrecognized officially), stepped outside the tent to adjust his revolver, then re-entered the tent and admitted authorship. Custer walked out. The issue would remain an open boil until a hot Sunday afternoon on the Little Bighorn seven years later.

Custer returned to headquarters at Fort Leavenworth, and his Libbie, in early April. They stayed there for several weeks, relaxing and enjoying the social life, before traveling west via the Kansas Pacific Railroad to Fort Hays to rejoin the Seventh Cavalry. They settled into the regiment's campsite, two miles east of the fort on Big Creek, and spent the summer and fall there. The post commander, General Nelson A. Miles, became a good friend, and he provided them with several large tents, which were set away from the rest of the regiment. The companies of the Seventh were sent out one by one to garrison posts along the Kansas Pacific's line. The nominal commander of the regiment, Colonel Smith, retired and was succeeded in June by Colonel Samuel D. Sturgis, who remained in Fort Leavenworth. Except for isolated visits that lasted a few weeks at most, he would rarely interfere with Custer's field command of the Seventh. Though he and Custer didn't get along owing to an 1865 dispute over supply contracts, he praised Custer to his superiors that year: "There is, perhaps, no other officer of equal rank on this line who has worked more faithfully against the Indians, or who has acquired the same degree of knowledge of the country and of the Indian character."

That summer Major Marcus A. Reno was assigned to the Seventh as the senior subordinate, a decision that didn't overjoy Custer. The short, stout Reno, a West Point graduate who had been brevetted a brigadier general during the war, had known Custer since he had served as a staff officer in the cavalry corps, but Custer—and, it appears, most of the Seventh's officers and men—thought little of his leadership abilities. The older Reno, for that matter, had little respect for Custer. Like many soldiers of the day, Reno was too fond of the bottle, and it would prove to be his downfall.

"Long Hair," as the Indians now called Custer, had little to do at Fort Hays, except for the occasional discipline problem. He and Libbie enjoyed a pleasant summer. Nights they would often go horseback riding together, and during the days Custer escorted luminaries and friends on buffalo hunts. He had gained a reputation as a buffalo hunter and sportsman largely on the strength of several articles he'd written for popular hunting journals, and he received hundreds of requests to guide hunting expeditions.

In October, the Custers returned to Fort Leavenworth as he had requested assignment to the larger post for the winter. A few weeks later Custer departed by train to visit friends and family in the East on a twenty-day leave that was extended to two months, and spent the Christmas holidays in Monroe. He returned to Leavenworth in mid-January 1870. In April, he was ordered with five companies of the Seventh to return to Fort Hays. Indian raids in the area west of

Major Marcus A. Reno
A brevet colonel during the Civil War, Reno joined the Seventh Cavalry in 1869.

Custer's Demand
Artist Charles C. Schreyvogel's 1903 oil painting of the meeting that secured the surrender of the Kiowa tribes and ended Sheridan's Indian campaign. Kiowa chiefs, from left, Little Heart, Lone Wolf, Kicking Bird, and Satanta met with scout and interpreter Grover, Lieutenant Colonel Custer, and Lieutenants Tom Custer and J. Schuyler Crosby in December 1868. Sheridan oversaw the proceedings from the background on the right. Frederic Remington later challenged the accuracy and artistic merit of the painting, which was staunchly defended by Crosby, who said that the only inaccuracy was the wrong shade of blue in his trousers.

there had increased of late, and a stronger military presence was needed. The attackers, however, were not intimidated by the operations of the depleted cavalry.

In the fall it was back to Leavenworth for Custer and his wife. He spent most of 1871 on extended leave in the East. From Monroe that spring and summer he visited New York to pursue various business prospects, particularly a silver-mining scheme in Colorado for which he pursued and landed several wealthy men and their money. The enterprise would eventually fail a few years later, but he spent the time socializing in the city's highest circles and exploring alternatives to continued military service—especially since his chances for promotion seemed dim. At the end of the summer he reported for duty at Louisville, Kentucky. The Seventh was assigned Reconstruction duty, and its companies were scattered throughout most of the Southern states. Custer and Company A were stationed forty miles south of Louisville in Elizabethtown.

The Custers remained in Elizabethtown for a year and a half. Custer disliked the political nature of the assignment, and his duty largely consisted of assisting federal peace officers with law enforcement, particularly in breaking the terroristic hold of the Ku Klux Klan. He was assigned to inspect horses bought for the cavalry, which he enjoyed, but it was for the most part a period of dullness and inactivity, and the Custers made frequent visits to Monroe and southern cities close by. The highlight of Custer's time there was a trip spent far away—on a buffalo hunt organized by Sheridan for Russian Grand Duke Alexis Alexandrovich Romanov,

Major General Phil Sheridan was convinced that the completion of the Northern Pacific Railroad through Montana and Wyoming and into the Pacific Northwest would "help to bring the Indian problem to a final solution."

"Lonesome" Charley Reynolds

Reynolds scouted for Custer during the Yellowstone and Black Hills Expeditions, and died during the Battle at the Little Bighorn. He was rumored to be a gentleman by birth.

Fort Rice, but Custer had allowed him to come along. Custer's insubordination in that matter and others infuriated Stanley, who called him "a cold-blooded, untruthful and unprincipled man" who was "universally despised by all the officers of his regiment excepting his relatives and one or two sycophants." Custer's heavy stove, he wrote, "delays the march often by his extensive packing up in the morning. . . . I will try, but I am not sure I can avoid trouble." Custer thought Stanley an undependable drunk and a humorless human being, which he was, but Custer's flouting of rank went too far. When Custer marched fifteen miles away from the column one day, Stanley decided to put his foot down. He reprimanded Custer and forbade him to leave again without orders. He also told Custer to consider himself under arrest, and ordered him to take his cavalry and march at the dusty rear of the column. Custer accepted the rebuke amiably. A few days later a sober Stanley released Custer from arrest and apologized, and once again Custer and his men were leading the way. The two got along well enough for the remainder of the expedition, and both subsequently spoke highly of each other in their letters home. Stanley believed he had established his authority, and Custer had apparently learned his lesson. But Stanley continued to drink heavily, and Custer took on more of the actual leadership as the march continued.

When the column caught up to the survey party, it turned out that Tom Rosser, Custer's West Point classmate and frequent foe during the Shenandoah campaign, was the Northern Pacific's chief engineer. The two had a high old time, sharing war stories long into the night.

They reached the Yellowstone in Montana Territory on July 14 and found the *Far West* waiting with supplies and mail. Fred Grant decided to return early to Washington upon hearing of his grandfather's death. A supply stockade was built and garrisoned with two companies of the Seventh, and the column continued westward a week later. The cavalry again led the way, followed by the team of surveyors and then the infantry. They were heading deep into Lakota land, where few if any white men had gone before. It was slow going over the rough terrain as a roadway had to be cut for the supply train. They reached the Powder River on July 31, and the Tongue four days later.

There, opposite the mouth of the Tongue, Custer and an advance squadron of ninety troopers dismounted for a noon break. They had just removed their saddles and begun to relax when a shot was heard. Upstream, they saw six Lakota warriors on horseback trying to stampede their horses. The guards repelled them, and the Indians retreated out of range. Custer and a small detachment of men mounted and rode toward them. The Indians galloped forward, then dashed away, again and again—a common ploy that Custer had seen before. He took two volunteers on fast mounts and rode forward, then halted, expecting an ambush.

The Curious Case of Mrs. Nash

ach Army company at a fort hired its own tailor, barber, and sometimes even blacksmith, and each troop also appointed its own laundress. Most were married to an officer or trooper, though a few were unmarried. Some single laundresses did more than wash clothes for the few dollars a month each man paid them; they catered to, in the words of one officer, "other wants of the men of a company than washing clothes." Most laundresses were helpful in other ways as well, often filling the roles of nurse, seamstress, cook, and midwife.

One of these women attached to Custer's Seventh Cavalry was a Mrs. Nash. She joined the regiment while it was assigned to Reconstruction duty in Kentucky in the early 1870s, and followed it north to Kansas in spring 1873. She almost always wore a veil or a shawl beneath her chin, and was described as rather peculiar-looking. She married a smiling quartermaster clerk named Clifton whose demeanor took a turn for the worse after the wedding. He deserted a few days before his enlistment expired.

Her next—and last— husband was a Private Noonan. But Mrs. Nash took sick and died while Noonan was out chasing Lakota with the regiment. Before she passed away, she asked that she be buried without being washed and dressed. Her friends refused, and when they undressed her they found that she was a he. Said Custer's orderly, John Burkman, "We was flabbergasted."

After Noonan returned, he insisted that his wife was female to anyone who would listen. But his mood gradually grew darker, and he avoided his comrades, who were all too happy to do the same. Not long after, he took a gun and shot himself in the heart. Said the *Bismarck Tribune*, "There was a sigh of relief on the corporate lips of the 7th Cavalry when its members heard that Noonan by his own hand had relieved the regiment of the odium which the man's presence cast upon them."

Custer and Private Noonan

Private Noonan, the unfortunate final husband of Mrs. Nash, stands immediately behind Custer on the occasion of Custer's first grizzly bear trophy in the Black Hills in April 1874. Bloody Knife kneels to the left of Custer; Captain William Ludlow stands on the right.

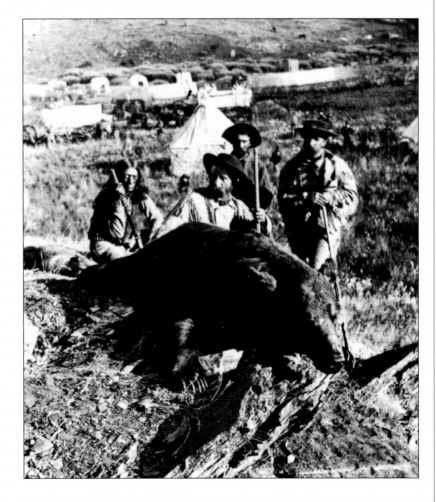

He wasn't disappointed. From cottonwoods along the river 300 Lakota and Cheyenne braves burst into view, yelling and firing as they attacked. Custer and men turned and galloped at full speed back to the detachment. The squadron joined them minutes later. The troopers dismounted in tall grass and dived to the ground. Just as the Indians reached them a line of cavalrymen stood and delivered a volley of carbine fire. That broke the initial charge, but the Indians circled the soldiers, firing into them. Custer was outnumbered three to one, but the numbers didn't worry him; a more serious problem was their meager ammunition. After a few hours of fighting, Custer decided on a tactic that had always worked for him before. He ordered his men to mount, then led them in a charge into the enemy. The Indians scattered, confirming his belief that a well-armed, disciplined squad of cavalry could break a larger Indian force.

One trooper was dead and another missing; in the search for him they found the bodies of the column's veterinarian and sutler. The two had apparently wandered off from the expedition and met up with the Lakota before the attack. The Seventh tracked the hostiles for the next five days, with Stanley and the infantry trailing behind.

When they reached the point where the Big Horn River met the Yellowstone, Custer spent two days trying to ford the deep, swirling river, but the horses refused to cross. At dawn on August 11, just before the cavalrymen tried again, Indians appeared on the bluffs on the opposite side of the river. They came down toward the Rosebud's banks and began shooting from a grove of cottonwoods on the far shore. On the crest of the bluffs behind them, the old men, women, and children of the village gathered to watch Long Hair and his men die. Custer ordered his troopers into a stand of timber set back from the river, where they began returning fire. Hearing shots from the cliffs on their side of the river, they realized Indians had crossed above and below the ford. They were surrounded.

Soon the rifle exchange was constant and fierce, and a few soldiers dropped to the ground. Custer deployed his sharpshooters and sent flanking support squadrons out. Hundreds of mounted Indians attacked several times; each time they were fought off. Custer then ordered his brother Tom to lead three companies in a counterattack into the Lakota. The regiment's band had accompanied the column, and they broke into "Garryowen." The Indians again retreated, crossing the river to safety as the infantry under Stanley came into view. He quickly deployed the battery of artillery, and their shells scattered the Indian riflemen across the river. The Seventh's losses were four men killed and four wounded. The Indians moved their camp south, and there were no further skirmishes.

A few days later the surveyors completed their work, and the expedition turned around to began the long journey east. Custer rode his men hard on the return trip, and they responded by calling

Custer the Hunter

Custer poses with an elk he shot during the Yellowstone Expedition. He was a passionate hunter and became a skilled taxidermist.

Custer With Saber
A few months before setting out on the Yellowstone Expedition, Custer sat for this photo in Memphis, Tennessee, in March 1873.

him "Hard Ass," a nod to his tirelessness in the saddle. The indefatigable Custer never seemed to understand that few soldiers owned his stamina, and fewer had the luxury of changing to a fresh mount as he did. The weary regiment rode into "Stanley's Stockade"—Camp Supply—on September 4. They waited for Stanley and the main column, then rode to Fort Abraham Lincoln near Bismarck, arriving on September 21.

The expedition was judged a success on all counts, and Custer's Indian-fighting and hunting exploits on the Yellowstone were reported almost daily in the Eastern papers. He was a front-page hero yet again. Stanley, the actual commander of the expedition, received only cursory mention. But that same day, the closing of the New York Stock Exchange and many banks precipitated the Panic of 1873. It was the country's first great economic depression. One of the many firms that declared bankruptcy was the Northern Pacific Railroad. There would be no railway construction, nor the settlement that went along with it, in the near future.

spirits. Few white men had ventured into this mysterious region. If a strategically located fort were to be built, the area would first have to be explored. Sheridan picked his old friend Custer to lead the Black Hills Expedition of 1874.

The official objective of the Expedition was reconnaissance, to scout for a suitable location for Sheridan's fort. But a secondary purpose, one never officially acknowledged but present just the same, would affect the course of the Sioux War even more significantly.

Since the California Gold Rush a quarter-century before, gold strikes in many western territories and the Pacific Northwest had resulted in massive waves of emigration. For years there had been rumors of gold in the Black Hills, but Indians had jealously guarded against any white intrusion into the area. Furthermore, the Treaty of 1868 specifically named the Black Hills as Indian country, part of the Great Sioux Reservation. Whites were not allowed to enter. But the Panic of 1873's depression motivated a desperate government to open up this El Dorado to settlers and miners; though the army attempted to prevent them from trespassing, it was often only token resistance.

So along with Custer's expedition and the engineers and surveyors preparing to take the measure of the Hills were two "practical miners" who would look for gold. Also on the trip would be three journalists and a top-notch photographer, two infantry companies, three Gatling guns, and a cannon. The soft-spoken "Lonesome" Charley Reynolds once more was Custer's chief guide. Colonel Fred Grant would again accompany Custer as a staff officer, and even the youngest Custer brother, Boston, had been signed up as a civilian forage master.

On July 2, 1874, the expedition marched out of Fort Lincoln to the strains of "The Girl I Left Behind Me" being played by the regimental band. A supply train of 100 wagons brought up the rear of

Divertissement

A typical afternoon's entertainment in the parlor of the Custer home at Fort Lincoln, July 1875. From left: Boston Custer, Margaret Calhoun, Lieutenant Winfield Edgerly, Libbie, Leonard Swett, Lieutenant R. Thompson, Nellie Wadsworth, Lieutenant Tom Custer, Custer, Emma Wadsworth, and Emily Watson.

At Home at Fort Lincoln

Custer and his family and friends pose on the porch of his first house at Fort Abraham Lincoln in November 1873. This house later burned down and was replaced by a much more elaborate structure.

Custer in His Study

Custer surrounded himself with animals he had hunted and stuffed himself, sculptures by Remington, his favorite photo of himself, a picture of Libbie in her wedding dress, and photo of his friend and commander General Sheridan. Custer wrote his memoirs, My Life on the Plains, *at this table in his study. He insisted that Libbie sit with him while he wrote.*

Custer and Friends

Custer poses with his family, friends, and officers at Fort Lincoln in November 1873. From left: Lieutenant Nelson Bronson, Lieutenant George D. Wallace, Custer, Lieutenant Benjamin H. Hodgson, Libbie, Mrs. Thomas McDougall, Lieutenant Thomas M. McDougall, Dr. J. V. T. Middleton, Annie Yates, Captain George W. Yates, Charles W. Thompson, Margaret Calhoun, Agnes Bates, Captain John S. Poland, Lieutenant Charles Varnum, Lieutenant Colonel William P. Carlin, Mrs. Myles Moylan, Lieutenant Tom Custer, Captain William Thompson, Lieutenant James Calhoun, Mrs. Donald McIntosh, Lieutenant Myles Moylan, and Lieutenant Donald McIntosh.

Horatio N. Ross

Ross was one of the two miners on the Black Hills Expedition that made the initial gold discovery.

the column, which consisted of more than a thousand men. If the Indians wanted trouble, Custer was ready.

After two weeks of a hot, dusty trek over the Plains, the expedition entered the Black Hills. Soon they encountered the only Indians of the trip: twenty-seven Oglala Lakota, up from a reservation on a hunting trip. The meeting was peaceful, though the Oglala fled after the Arikara scouts, their traditional enemies, threatened them. As the excursion worked its way south, it developed into a combination picnic and hunting party. Again Custer hunted and gathered fossils by day and practiced his taxidermy and wrote by night. He shot his first grizzly, though his orderly and Bloody Knife also hit the beast.

The miners panned many streams without luck until July 30, 1874, when they found small traces of gold in French Creek. When they confirmed steady but unspectacular deposits a few days later, Custer asked for a volunteer to carry dispatches to Fort Laramie in Wyoming Territory, 150 miles distant and through dangerous Indian country. Only Reynolds volunteered. Traveling just at night, with only a compass to guide him, he reached the fort a few days later with the good news. After another week of exploring, with French Creek as a base camp, Custer marched his men back to Fort Lincoln. On the way he camped next to Bear Butte just clear of the Black Hills, where Fort Meade would be built in 1878.

The column paraded into Fort Lincoln on August 30 to find the entire country excited at the news of Black Hills gold. Despite Custer's uncharacteristic restraint and caution in his early descriptions of the gold strikes—"until further examination is made regarding the richness of gold, no opinion should be formed"—newspapers all over the country loudly proclaimed the good news.

Pack Train

Custer's pack train winds through a Dakota valley on the Black Hills Expedition of 1874.

"Rich Mines of Gold and Silver Reported Found by Custer," announced one; another predicted the region would become "the El Dorado of America." The *Chicago Inter-Ocean*'s headline trumpeted: "The Precious Dust Found in the Grass Under the Horses' Feet—Excitement Among the Troops." Soon Custer himself had

Above: **Expedition Camp**

Custer's camp at Hiddenwood Creek in the Black Hills.

Above: **"Gold!"**

Although the prospectors in Custer's Black Hills Expedition only found small amounts of gold, the announcement caused a furor in the Eastern press, such as these headlines in the Chicago Inter-Ocean from August 27, 1874, and spurred a massive gold rush. The army and the government gave up trying to keep out miners from the Black Hills, which had been designated as an Indian reservation.

Left: **Custer and Scouts**

Custer and his Ree Indian scouts plan their route during the Black Hills Expedition in August 1874. His chief and favorite scout, Bloody Knife, kneels to the left of Custer and points at the map; Goose stands behind Custer. The other two scouts are unidentified.

Indian Identity Certificate
Certificates such as this one, issued to the Oglala chief Old Man Afraid of His Horses, were issued to treaty Indians to travel to and from the Black Hills reservation at will. As the certificate stated, the bearer's "influence has been to preserve peace and harmony" and "is entitled to the confidence of all persons whom he may meet."

succumbed to the fever, and was speaking of the gold deposits in glowing terms. The report triggered a Gold Rush to the area, and by summer 1875, there were more than a thousand miners roaming the sacred grounds of the Lakota. In support of the Treaty of 1868, the government warned the miners against trespassing and ordered them to leave, but the army performed its duties halfheartedly and looked the other way when the miners returned. When another Black Hills expedition that year confirmed gold deposits in the region, the trickle of emigration became a flood.

In September, a government commission was sent to negotiate with the Lakota for the sale of the Black Hills. Many of the older leaders were ready to deal. But younger nontreaty Lakota, outraged by Custer's blazing of the "Thieves' Road" into the area and the continued presence of white men there, rode onto the reservation and threatened their elders with death if they signed. The negotiations went badly, and the commission returned to Washington

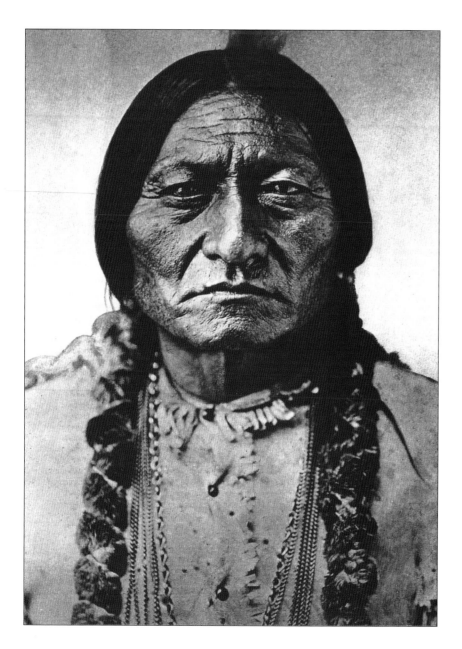

Sitting Bull

The charismatic Sitting Bull's influence extended far beyond his own Lakota tribe. A fierce warrior in his youth, he became neither a chief nor a war leader of the Hunkpapas but a respected medicine man. Sitting Bull became the political and spiritual leader of the Northern Plains Indians and unified the northern tribes in their resistance to the "white man's road."

Far left: Secretary of War William W. Belknap

Belknap resigned amid mounting evidence of governmental corruption, an event that many American citizens felt had tarnished the national character.

Left: President Ulysses S. Grant

Grant was furious over Custer's criticism of his administration and policies.

Above: **Taxidermist**

In the 1870s, the Kansas Pacific Railway operated its own taxidermy shop so buffalo hunters shooting from its trains could have a place to mount buffalo trophies.

Right: **Mountain of Buffalo Skulls**

From 1872 to 1874, one million buffalo were killed annually, most of them by hide hunters. According to General Sheridan, the buffalo hunters were doing "more to settle the vexed Indian question than the entire regular Army has done in the last thirty years."

on charges that Secretary of War William W. Belknap had received bribes and kickbacks from his army-post tradership appointments. Though a guilty Belknap resigned when evidence mounted that he had accepted $20,000 in graft, the Democratic committee was eager to root out even more crooked Grant appointees in an election year. Grant was personally honest and above reproach, but he was a bad judge of friends and acquaintances, and his administration was one of the most corrupt in American history.

An adamant Democrat, Custer was a frequent contributor to anti-Grant journals, and was known as a vocal critic of the post sutler system. Since he had to buy from the posts as well, Custer had first-hand experience of the outrageous prices charged to troopers, who were barred from purchasing elsewhere. Additionally, the usually magnanimous Custer had hated Belknap since the War Secretary had overruled Custer in an argument with a post sutler. Thus, he was an attractive witness.

However, the last thing Custer wanted was to travel to Washington at this time. Terry had promised Custer the honor of rounding up the renegade Indians in the spring, and in January, Custer wrote his brother: "I think the 7th cavalry may have its greatest mission ahead." Custer attempted to avoid the trip to the capital by offering to answer Congress's questions in writing, but his offer was refused, and he arrived in Washington to testify at the end of March. His wooing by leading Democrats apparently led him to forget his last experience with politics, the unpleasant "Swing Around the Circle" with President Johnson in 1866. Though his unsubstantiated evidence was ruled out as hearsay, it was headline material as he implicated the President's brother, Orvil Grant, and others. President Grant was already angered by Custer's criticism of his Indian policy in *My Life on the Plains*, a collection of Custer's magazine articles published in 1874. Now he hit the ceiling and directed his new secretary of war to assign another commander to the upcoming campaign.

Custer was aware of Grant's fury but knew nothing of Grant's plan to replace him. Still, Sherman advised him to call on the President personally to patch things up. Custer went to the White House several times, but Grant refused to see him; on the final

Picnic
Custer, Libbie, and friends on an 1875 picnic in Dakota Territory. Custer stands in front of the center pole, Libbie seated to the left of him.

Charades at Fort Lincoln
Custer and Agnes Bates, a close friend of Libbie's, dress up as a Lakota chief and his daughter in the summer of 1875.

General Alfred Terry

Terry served as commander of the Department of the Dakota Territory.

Colonel John Gibbon

Gibbon was a brevet major general during the Civil War. His command was dubbed the Iron Brigade for their indestructibility at South Mountain, Virginia.

occasion, he allowed Custer to cool his heels in an antechamber for five hours. Custer left the capital on the night of May 1, visited his parents in Monroe, and then headed to Chicago to continue west. At the Chicago railroad station on his way to St. Paul, he was met by an army officer with a telegram from Sherman. Grant, on a flimsy pretext, ordered Custer detained and dropped from the expedition. Custer wired Sherman, explaining what had happened in Washington, and received Sherman's permission to proceed to staff headquarters in St. Paul. There, a tearful Custer begged General Terry—a thoughtful, compassionate man—to help him. Terry had been named the column's new field commander, and he knew he'd need Custer's expertise. He helped Custer compose a message to the president. "I appeal to you as a soldier," it read, "to spare me the humiliation of seeing my regiment march to meet the enemy and I not share its dangers." Sheridan, though furious at his friend's foolish testimony, advised Grant that Custer was vital to the campaign's success. On May 8, the President reinstated Custer, though he would now only command the Seventh Cavalry instead of the entire column, which would be lead by Terry.

That was an insignificant detail to Custer: He had gotten free of Stanley three years ago during the Northern Pacific survey, and he felt confident he could do the same now. Custer was also sure that a victory over the large group of Indians gathered in the Powder River country would put him back in Grant's good graces. And if the Democrats captured the White House in the upcoming election, a brigadier general's star was possible. The president appointed generals, and the Democrats owed Custer. Yes, this was a golden opportunity—and perhaps the last great Indian battle ever. He wouldn't have missed it for the world.

The hostile Indian camp on the Rosebud Creek in spring 1876 may have been the largest Indian gathering the Northern Plains had ever seen. The population of the hostile camps always swelled in the spring when other Indians from the agencies joined them, but this year there were even more. Thousands of angry Indians had heeded Sitting Bull's call to arms and left their reservations for one last big fight with the *wasichus*. Crazy Horse had led his band of Oglalas 200 miles north in February to join Sitting Bull's Hunkpapas, and several other groups followed, if only for protection. Most of the Indians knew that their days roaming the Plains were numbered, though Sitting Bull and Crazy Horse talked of a fight to the last man that might last another ten years.

Sitting Bull had been a fierce warrior in his youth, but he was neither a chief nor a war leader of the Hunkpapas. He was a well-respected medicine man and easily the most influential of the Lakota. Through his intelligence, forceful personality, and compassion—and his disdain for the "white man's road"—he had become·

the political and spiritual leader of the Northern Plains Indians. More than any other Indian, he was responsible for the unification of the various northern tribes, and their continued resistance to the white man.

The enigmatic Crazy Horse was something different entirely. Though younger than Sitting Bull—Crazy Horse was born in the same year as Custer, 1839—he was a respected warrior, and after Red Cloud left for the reservation, he became the de facto war leader of the Oglalas. His bravery and skill in leading war parties was unrivaled. A small white stone he wore as a charm was thought to give him great medicine, and he was never injured despite taking extraordinary risks.

Crazy Horse was more than just a ferocious warrior, however; he was also known as a storyteller and teacher. He cared little for the trappings and honors of success. He was one of only a few head men in his tribe selected as a Shirt-wearer by the tribal council for his leadership skills. This honor made him responsible for the welfare of his people, and he became as well-known for his charity as for his courage, keeping nothing for himself except his weapons and a few necessities, and providing for the weak and helpless. The ceremonial Shirt-wearer shirt he was given was decorated with human hair from the people of the tribe. Though only of average height and build, he radiated a charisma that few other leaders, white or Indian, could match. He had light skin and light hair, a sharp nose, and a thinner face than most Oglalas, and as a young boy whites often mistook him for a captive white child. There was an almost mystical aura about him which was furthered by his refusal to play the white man's game—he refused to be photographed, and avoided any contact with the *wasichus*. Like Sitting Bull, he had vowed to fight to the bitter end.

But the Indians' reality was painful. Not only was the army hunting them down relentlessly, but the sacred buffalo, which provided for so many of their needs, was being exterminated at the astonishing rate of one million a year by professional hunters. The summer of 1876 would probably be the last breath of their traditional way of life. A Sun Dance—a religious ceremony of the Plains tribes—would be held, buffalo and antelope would be hunted, and the tribes would get together one last time. It was too much to resist for many reservation Indians, particularly young men who craved a chance to count coup and prove themselves on the hunt and in battle, and court the young maidens.

So the various Lakota tribes streamed into camp, including more Oglalas from Red Cloud Agency and Brules from Spotted Tail Agency—both in Nebraska—Blackfeet from the western Dakota Territory, Santees from the Missouri River, Sans Arcs, and even some Assiniboines and Arapahoes. Fifty lodges of Cheyenne from Red Cloud Agency came as well. All told, by the third week in June there

Boston Custer
The youngest Custer brother, Boston joined Armstrong and Tom in the Dakota Territory as a civilian forage scout.

Henry Armstrong "Autie" Reed
Custer's favorite nephew, Reed rode with the Seventh Cavalry for the thrills; he was on the payroll as a beef herder. He died with his three uncles at the Battle of the Little Bighorn when he was only eighteen years old.

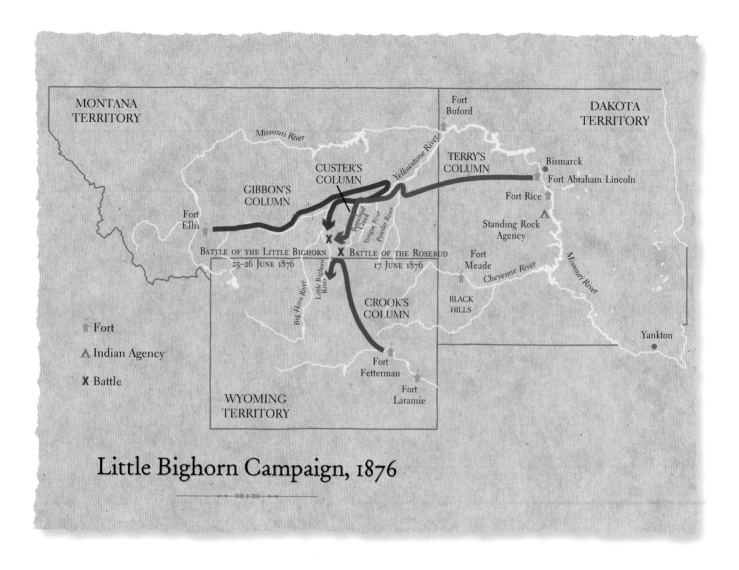

Little Bighorn Campaign, 1876

were at least 1,000 lodges and 7,000 Indians there—and probably close to 2,000 of them were well-armed warriors, at least half carrying guns.

The massive encampment had to move every few days to find enough spring grass for the 10,000-strong pony herd, but buffalo were plentiful. In early June, they moved to the Little Bighorn Valley in Montana Territory, then back to the Rosebud, where the traditional Sun Dance was held on June 6. Sitting Bull participated, and had a vision of soldiers "falling right into our camp." The revelation pleased the Lakota. It was an omen they would remember for a long time.

Meanwhile, the three army columns were wending their way toward the Indian camp. Gibbon's 400 infantry and Terry's 1,000-strong column would meet at a site on the Yellowstone six miles above the mouth of Rosebud Creek in Montana Territory, while Crook's 1,300 men approached from the south. Though the overall strategy was to surround the enemy, no plans were made to attack the Indians in

Seventh Cavalry Troopers

A cadre of unidentified Seventh Cavalry troopers, photographed at Fort Lincoln just prior to riding west with Custer on their last campaign.

concert, and any such plans would have been foolish and impractical; communication was difficult, the country and terrain unknown, and no one knew where or how big the Indian camp was. Each leader was confident that his column had sufficient manpower and firepower to handle the Indians, no matter how many there were. And since this was likely the last great Indian battle, each wanted to strike the Indians alone. The victorious commander in this fight would likely go down in history as the greatest Indian fighter in America's history.

Terry's column left Fort Lincoln at dawn on May 17, 1876. A fog hung in the air as the Seventh Cavalry band played "Garryowen" and then "The Girl I Left Behind Me." Wives waved goodbye as the two-mile column moved out. Libbie and her sister-in-law Maggie traveled with their husbands that first day's march, then returned to Lincoln the next morning with the paymaster, who had accompanied the column in order to pay the men away from the fleshpots of Bismarck.

General George Crook

Custer, wearing fringed buckskins, a dark-blue flannel blouse, red tie, broad-brimmed, cream-colored slouch hat, and shorn locks, was leading his beloved Seventh over the Great Plains toward a confrontation with an enemy army. He was jubilant, especially since he was accompanied by many of the Custer "family": his two brothers, Tom and Boston; his teenage nephew, Henry Armstrong "Autie" Reed, along for the excitement and on the payroll as a beef herder; his brother-in-law, Lieutenant Calhoun; and other favorite officers, such as Yates, Moylan, Cooke, Weir, and A. E. "Fresh" Smith. A newspaperman from the *Bismarck Tribune*, Mark Kellogg, rode along and joined the Custer circle, as did several others. Some of Custer's dogs trotted alongside the column. Only Libbie was missing. In her absence the practical joker in Custer held sway, with Boston as the frequent target. Custer often disappeared on extended hunting trips. At night he wrote deep into the evening, then woke up early to finish his correspondence.

The Seventh was considered one of the army's finest fighting units, and its record was undeniable. But cracks were beginning to show. Thirteen line officers—two majors, four captains, and seven lieutenants—were missing on leave or detached service. Thus the chain of command was weakened, with fewer experienced officers and replacements who were still getting to know their men. Sixty-two of the regiment's troopers were green recruits, in the field only two months, and almost 100 more had only six months' training. Many of them were poor horsemen and, since practice rounds were rarely issued and target practice was infrequent, even poorer shots. Some enlisted men had never fired their carbines and had only the vaguest idea of how to work their weapons. Many of the horses were green also, with little or no experience in battle, under fire, or with Indians.

And of course, there was the Custer schism within the veteran officer corps. Custer's highest-ranking officers, Major Marcus Reno and Captain Frederick Benteen, both despised their CO—and didn't get along themselves. Despite his honorable Civil War record, the short, swarthy Reno was an ineffectual leader who commanded little respect from his superiors or the men beneath him. When Custer had been in Grant's disfavor, Reno had lobbied for command of the regiment on the march against the Lakota; Terry had ignored him. Reno was a leader in rank only, and a man who seems to have gone through life with a cloud over his head. Bad luck seemed to find him; at first it was circumstantial, but increasingly it was due to his actions. He was also cold and socially inept. He disliked Custer and envied him his friends, his rank, and his fame.

The senior captain, Benteen, was the more intelligent—and more interesting—of the two. Born into an upper-class Virginia family, he was a fearless soldier, courageous in battle, and had been an exceptional leader during the Civil War, commanding a regiment toward its end. He was also a good husband and loving father to Freddie, his only surviving child; he and his wife had lost four other

Above: Battle of the Rosebud

Celebrated Indian fighter Crook almost met his own fate just days before the Battle of the Little Bighorn. On June 17, 1876, Crook's cavalry was surrounded by 1,000 Lakota and Cheyenne warriors, led by Crazy Horse, at the Battle of the Rosebud in Montana Territory. They barely escaped with their lives. This woodcut was made of a sketch by James E. Taylor.

Right: Washakie

At the Battle of the Rosebud, valiant fighting by the cavalry's 200 Shoshone allies, led by chief Washakie, bought valuable time for Crook's command.

THE CUSTER ZOO

It is doubtful—or at least unrecorded—that any officer of the U.S. Army owned a stronger passion for animals than George Armstrong Custer. At varying times on the Plains, Custer's menagerie included wolves, a porcupine, beaver, wildcat, goats, squirrels, and even a pelican. Custer had a pet field mouse that crawled over his papers and arms and shoulders as he wrote his memoirs during the winter of 1875, and a raccoon that slept in the Custer bed at night, to the consternation of Libbie. He even made pets of antelopes: At one time he had five of them in camp that would wander about looking for Custer or his wife, and Libbie tells of a group of astonished Indians who watched as one antelope bounded into the general's tent, interrupting a meeting with a demand for petting. Custer was of course an excellent equestrian, and a good judge of horseflesh (for several months in the early 1870s he was given the job of inspecting Army horse purchases). Few things in life gave him more pleasure than riding across the Plains for hours at a time on one of his thoroughbreds.

But nothing gave Custer more pleasure than his dogs. At Fort Lincoln, he had kennels at the back of his quarters filled with the finest breeds of fox and stag hounds. He bragged frequently in letters to his wife of his hunting dogs' performance and waxed ecstatic when two of them killed a wolf. At his posts on the Plains he seemed always to be accompanied by eight or ten of them, and if he threw himself on the ground he was soon at the bottom of a mound of hound. In *Boots and Saddles*, Libbie wrote that when the puppies were let inside the tent in bad weather, her husband would ask that "the hound that had fits" be allowed in, then one or another "that had been hurt in hunting," and so on, until the tent overflowed with wet, smelly dogs. When one of his many dogs was sick, particularly a puppy, "he walked the floor half the night, holding, rubbing, trying to soothe the suffering little beast." He carried

Custer and Menagerie

Custer outside his tent at Fort Dodge, Kansas, in November 1868 with his Spencer carbine, his hunting dogs, and his pet pelican that he captured on the Arkansas River.

with him a book on dog medicine that he referred to frequently. When returning from a hunt, he often doctored his hunting dogs before shedding his jacket.

The childless Custers seemed to surround themselves with animals as surrogate children. When one favorite staghound died, Custer grieved deeply, even writing an elegy (with lines borrowed from poet Lord Byron) for her.

Ironically, Custer was often kinder and more responsive to his dogs than he was to his men: On the march back over the Great Plains from the Black Hills in 1874, Custer ordered some of his enlisted men to get out of the ambulance wagon and walk so his staghounds, whose feet were sore, could ride.

children to spinal meningitis. But his hatred for Custer was almost pathological; he would later admit that he had disliked the younger, more successful Custer from the start. There were many things about Custer that no doubt rankled: his superior rank, his relative youth, his academy training, his flamboyance, his boyish exuberance, his hunger for acclaim, his avoidance of drink and swearing, his Northern "pushiness"—all these and more surely contributed to Benteen's hatred for Custer.

Custer's Horses
Custer's orderly, Private John Burkman, holds Dandy (left) and Vic, Custer's two favorite mounts.

Actually, there didn't seem to be many people the cantankerous Benteen did like, though many of his men were loyal to him, partly due to his humane treatment of them. He got along badly with most of the other officers, and had little use for Reno, whom he had slapped one night in a bar. But the writing and publication of his Washita letter was ethically dubious at best, and it helped create the chasm in the Seventh's officers' ranks that would continue until the Little Bighorn.

Reno and Benteen were united in their contempt for Custer, however, and there were other officers in the Seventh who for one reason or another resented their commanding officer. Regardless of any personal animosity, they were professional soldiers who attempted to do their jobs as best they could. The next few days would test that dedication to the extreme.

"Lonesome" Charley Reynolds, one of Custer's most trusted scouts and a man well-liked by the others in spite of his quiet nature, guided the column. He had handled the same duties for the Stanley expedition three years earlier along the same route, so he knew the country—at least the first part of the journey, to the Yellowstone. The column included all twelve companies of the Seventh, three infantry companies, three Gatling guns, and a few hundred teamsters, civilians, and Indian scouts, including Custer's favorite, Bloody Knife. Thirty other Indian scouts, under the direction of Lieutenant Charles A. Varnum, accompanied them.

General Terry, on his first expedition over the Great Plains, was not overly enthusiastic about Custer's boyish shenanigans, or his penchant for disappearing most of the day, particularly an unauthorized forty-five-mile scout up the Little Missouri. Still, the sedentary, soft-spoken Terry was intelligent enough to know that he would need Custer when the column struck into unfamiliar territory—and when it came time to fight. Besides, he was more concerned with his

No one worried about whipping the hostiles. The army's experience was that a well-disciplined force of soldiers with superior firepower could conquer an Indian force several times its number. More than anything, they feared that they wouldn't find the Indians before they scattered in all directions.

comfort and cuisine, as his letters home readily attest. But on June 10, he assigned Reno, not Custer, command of a reconnaissance up the Powder and down the Tongue Valleys. Reno disobeyed Terry's precise instructions as to his route, but when he returned nine days later he brought valuable intelligence. He had struck a large trail and turned and followed it cross-country to the Rosebud, which he had followed down to the Yellowstone. The Indians were not on the lower Rosebud as expected.

The *Far West* had paddled up the Yellowstone to the rendezvous point at the mouth of the Tongue, and on June 21, Terry, Gibbon, Custer, and Major James Brisbin, in command of the Second Cavalry, conferred for two hours aboard the steamship. They had no idea where or how big the Indian camp was, and they were about to move into unknown territory. They decided that the Indian camp lay in either the valley of the Big Horn, Little Bighorn, or the upper Rosebud. They estimated 1,000 warriors at most. Terry outlined a plan.

To ensure capture of the hostiles before they could scatter, the commands would operate separately. Custer and the Seventh would march up the Rosebud, then descend along the Little Bighorn if the trail led that way. Gibbon, accompanied by Terry, his infantry, and Brisbin's cavalry, would advance up the Yellowstone to the mouth of the Big Horn, then follow that stream to the Little Bighorn. Terry expected Gibbon's force to be in place on or about June 26, but there was no set plan to coordinate any attack on that date. If either force encountered the Indians before then, they would attack, though it was assumed that Custer's more mobile strike force would be the lucky one, and rightly so. "I only hope that one of the two columns will find the Indians," Terry wrote Sheridan that morning. Gibbon's role was merely to block the northward escape of any Indians who got away from Custer, and to that end Terry offered Custer four Second Cavalry companies from Gibbon's command and the Gatling battery. Custer declined, saying that the heavy guns would only slow him up, and the 600 men of the Seventh could handle any Indians they ran into. No one worried about whipping the hostiles. The army's experience was that a well-disciplined force of soldiers with superior firepower could conquer an Indian force several times its number. More than anything, they feared that they wouldn't find the Indians before they scattered in all directions, as they had always done in the past.

Their plans might have changed had they known of recent events eighty miles to the south. On March 1, Crook captured a small Lakota-Cheyenne village and found an enormous cache of ammunition along with powder, piglead, and molds for casting bullets. The hostiles clearly appeared to be taking this latest threat upon them seriously, and near the end of spring they confirmed that stupendously. On June 17, 1876, a force of some 1,000 Lakota and Cheyenne, led by Crazy Horse, attacked Crook's column near the headwaters of the Rosebud in Montana Territory, determined to prevent the bluecoats from reaching their village. The soldiers were not prepared for an attack. The weary troopers had just finished an early-morning march and were unsaddling their horses and preparing coffee; Crook was playing cards with his officers. The Indians swooped down into the mile-wide Rosebud Valley from a high hill on the north side. If not for the bravery of Crook's 200 Shoshone scouts under the command of Washakie, who had specifically accompanied Crook hoping to fight their Lakota enemies, Crook's troops might have been overwhelmed. The Shoshone bought time for the troops, and the battle became a jumbled mass of several smaller battles, as the Indians rode again and again into the separated cavalry units. They were "charging boldly and rapidly through the soldiers, knocking them from their horses with lances and knives, dismounting and killing them," said one officer later. It was a dramatically different strategy for the Indians, who had always preferred to circle at a distance and draw the whites into ambushes. This day, they galloped straight into the cavalry lines with a fierceness that impressed even seasoned soldiers.

Crook counterattacked, but brilliant generalship by Crazy Horse and other leaders foiled the charge. Then Crook made the mistake of separating his force to attack a village he mistakenly thought was nearby, and only quick action prevented a flank attack by Crazy Horse from dividing and destroying his men. The fight became a back-and-forth affair among the ridges, hills, and valleys that rose up on either side of the Rosebud, until late in the afternoon when the Lakota withdrew. Crook held the field, and claimed a victory—"my troops beat these Indians on a field of their own choosing, and drove them in utter route from it," he said in his official report—but it was a hollow one. His ten dead and twenty-one wounded hindered his mobility, and his troops had used up most of their ammunition—25,000 rounds to kill an estimated ten Indians. Fearing an ambush if he headed north through a narrow canyon, Crook retreated south the next day and did not venture into the field again until mid-July. While Terry, Gibbon, and Custer strategized on the *Far West*, Crook's 1,300 men awaited reinforcements in their camp on Goose Creek in Wyoming Territory while their officers went fishing.

Terry, Gibbon, and Custer knew nothing of the Battle of the Rosebud when they met on June 22. They did not know that in a matter of days the Indian village would more than double to almost 10,000 strong as agency Indians streamed into camp, or that their success against Crook on the Rosebud had made them more confident than ever. Their determination to fight the white man rather than avoid him was at a peak. This time they would not run.

The Lakota were "charging boldly and rapidly through the soldiers, knocking them from their horses with lances and knives, dismounting and killing them," said one cavalry officer. It was a dramatically different strategy for the Indians.

In Battle Joined

"The largest Indian camp on the North American continent is ahead and I am going to attack it."
—George Armstrong Custer to his officers, June 25, 1876

At noon (Chicago time, which was kept at Fort Lincoln) on June 22, 1876, the Seventh Cavalry, the pride of the U.S. Army, marched south from the mouth of the Rosebud River, parading past Gibbon, Terry, and Custer. Spirits were high, for it seemed that the regiment would be the lucky one to strike the enemy first. In Custer's pocket were written orders from Terry delivered that morning that clarified the mission.

Reno's Charge
Minneconjou warrior Red Horse's pictograph painting depicts the initial Seventh Cavalry charge led by Major Reno being routed by the Lakota and Cheyenne at the Battle of the Little Bighorn.

Camp at Mouth of Rosebud River
Montana Territory
June 22, 1876

Colonel:

The Brigadier-General Commanding directs that, as soon as your regiment can be made ready for the march, you will proceed up the Rosebud in pursuit of the Indians whose trail was discovered by Major Reno a few days since. It is, of course, impossible to give you any definite instructions in regard to this movement, and were it not impossible to do so the Department Commander places too much confidence in your zeal, energy, and ability to wish to impose upon you precise orders which might hamper your action when nearly in contact with the enemy. He will, however, indicate to you his own views of what your actions should be, and he desires that you should conform to them unless you shall see sufficient reason for departing from them. He thinks that you should proceed up the Rosebud until you ascertain definitely the direction in which the trail above spoken of leads. Should it be found (as it appears almost certain that it will be found) to turn towards the Little Horn, he thinks that you should still proceed southward, perhaps as far as the headwaters of the Tongue, and then turn toward the Little Horn, feeling constantly, however, to your left, so as to preclude the escape of the Indians to the south or southeast by passing around your left flank. The column of Colonel Gibbon is now in motion for the mouth of the Big Horn. As soon as it reaches that point it will cross the Yellowstone and move up at least as far as the forks of the Big and Little Horns. Of course its future movements must be controlled by circumstances as they arise, but it is hoped that the Indians, if upon the Little Horn, may be so nearly inclosed by the two columns that their escape will be impossible.

The Department Commander desires that on your way up the Rosebud you should thoroughly examine the upper part of Tullock's Creek, and that you should endeavor to send a scout through to Colonel Gibbon's column with the information of the result of your examination. The lower part of this creek will be examined by a detachment from Colonel Gibbon's command. The supply steamer will be pushed up the Big Horn as far as the forks if the river is found to be navigable for that distance, and the Department Commander, who will accompany the column of Colonel Gibbon, desires you to report to him there not later than the expiration of the time for

Mitch Boyer

Boyer, a mixed-blood scout and interpreter, had been trained by legendary mountain man Jim Bridger. He rode to his death with Custer at the Little Bighorn.

which your troops are rationed, unless in the mean time you receive further orders.

Very respectfully
Your obedient servant,
E. W. Smith
Captain, 18th Infantry
Acting Assistant Adjutant General

As Custer took his leave and rode after his regiment, Gibbon called out to him: "Now, Custer, don't be greedy, but wait for us." Custer waved and called out over his shoulder, "No, I will not." An officer nearby later claimed to hear Terry say, "Custer is happy now, off with a roving command of fifteen days. I told him if he found the Indians not to do as Reno did [Reno had been rebuked for not pursuing the Indians after striking their trail on the scout up the Powder], but if he thought he could whip them to do so."

Custer led a below-strength Seventh Cavalry: 27 officers, around 575 enlisted men, 43 Indian scouts, and more than a dozen civilians, including interpreters Mitch Boyer, of mixed French and Lakota ancestry and one of the finest guides in the country; the well-respected Isaiah Dorman, the only black man on the expedition; and Frederick Gerard, a veteran trader who had been married to an Arikara woman. Boston Custer, Armstrong's youngest brother who was spending a season on the dry plains in hopes of improving the tuberculosis he suffered from, and George Herendeen, a dependable jack of all trades, were along as civilian guides. All told, there were about 650 men in the column, more than a few sporting the cooler straw hats they had bought recently from the expedition sutler. A train of 175 pack mules with rations for fifteen days and extra carbine ammunition followed, guided by civilian packers. Left behind were Custer's beloved dogs, the regiment's sabers and band, and the wagons.

They marched two miles up the Yellowstone, crossed the Rosebud, then rode ten miles upstream that afternoon, following the river's east bank, before Custer decided to bivouac, partly because of recurring problems with the pack train. The men saw to their mounts and prepared camp, and after supper Custer held officers' call. He outlined his plans and went over precautions concerning unnecessary noise, among other things. Before he closed the briefing, the normally brusque commander invited suggestions from them. He seemed uncharacteristically subdued and conciliatory, and more than one officer commented on it after the briefing. "He took particular pains to impress upon the officers his reliance upon their judgment, discretion, and loyalty," Lieutenant Godfrey recalled. "This 'talk' of his . . . was considered at the time something extraordinary for General Custer."

Frederick Gerard
Gerard was an able interpreter and trader who rode with the Seventh Cavalry.

Lieutenant Charles A. Varnum
Varnum was Custer's chief of scouts.

Seventh Cavalry Standard

This Seventh Cavalry regimental standard accompanied the troops to the Little Bighorn, but was kept with the pack train.

Goes Ahead

Goes Ahead was one of the Crow scouts who accompanied Custer at the Little Bighorn.

The next day, June 23, they broke camp before dawn and marched thirty-three miles, crossing and recrossing the Rosebud. They halted at three deserted campsites to inspect the Indian trail. Before noon they came upon the large lodge-pole trail that Reno had found and followed it until late afternoon. That evening, Custer sent his six Crow scouts borrowed from Gibbon's Seventh Infantry ahead to reconnoiter. With them went Boyer, who, next to his mentor Jim Bridger, was known as the finest scout in the country—so valuable that Sitting Bull was said to have offered a reward of 100 horses for his scalp. He had started the expedition with Gibbon but had been assigned with the Crows to Custer; they knew the country well, and as the strike force, the Seventh would need them far more than Gibbon.

The regiment was again on the march before dawn the next day, following the trail upstream twenty-seven miles. But they were no longer duplicating Reno's route; the path ahead was through unknown country. That morning they came upon the site of a large, deserted encampment. The unmistakable remains of a Sun Dance lodge still stood, and two white scalps were found. The Ree scouts sensed the significance of the lodge; they understood the renewal of hope, spirit, and confidence it represented. The grass for acres around had been cropped close to the ground by a huge pony herd. The regiment halted for an hour, then moved out. Further on, the

Crows returned to the column to report an even newer trail ahead, a fresh one no more than two days old.

They halted at 1 P.M. near another large, deserted campsite. The break lasted four hours while scouts reconnoitered several fresh trails and campsites. They moved out at 5 P.M. and followed the main trail, which now stretched a mile wide from one side of the valley to the other. The hostile Indian camp was close. Custer ordered Arikara flankers to be kept well out in search of lodge-pole trails leaving the main column. He still feared a break-up of the encampment. He wanted the whole village, every last lodge.

Just before 8 P.M. they bivouacked near the Rosebud in an Indian camp about two days old. The men grazed their animals and ate supper. Some of the officers gathered at Lieutenant Keogh's tent to tell stories and down some whiskey. Then, as darkness was falling, the Crow scouts returned with unexpected news. Just ahead the trail turned west and crept over the divide between the Rosebud and the Little Bighorn Valleys.

Custer immediately adjusted his plans. Then, by the light of a single candle, he met with his officers at his tent to tell them of his decision. The large village the army had been hunting for months was within striking distance, and the trail was so fresh that it had to be nearby on the lower Little Bighorn. To continue up the Rosebud would lead them further away from the enemy, and they would surely be detected. To risk losing the prize almost in their grasp made no sense. They would follow the trail over the divide that night, reconnoiter and rest the next day, then strike camp at dawn on June 26, when Gibbon was scheduled to reach the mouth of the Little Bighorn. A dawn attack on a sleeping village had worked brilliantly at the Washita, and Custer was confident it would work here.

Just before midnight the sleepy troopers broke camp, moving slowly uphill under a moonless sky. They followed a small stream six miles over rough terrain and halted at 3 A.M. in a sheltered hollow just short of the summit. Behind them lay the valley of the Rosebud. Just over the crest lay the valley of the Little Bighorn, or the Greasy Grass, as the Indians called the winding stream. The men attempted to catch up on their sleep as best they could, some just lying on the ground still holding their reins. The scattered pack train stumbled in a few hours later. There was not much grass for the horses, and the water was so alkaline that the horses wouldn't drink and the troopers spat out coffee made from it. Just after dawn, chief of scouts Varnum sent a message to Custer to join him with several of the white and Indian scouts. They had found the camp.

Custer joined them on a high, double-peaked ridge called the Crow's Nest, which commanded an excellent view of both valleys. They examined the landscape to the west. The Crows claimed they could see the village and the pony herd some fifteen miles away on

Hairy Moccasin
Hairy Moccasin was a Crow scout with Custer's battalion.

Rain-in-the-Face
The Hunkpapa Rain-in-the-Face was one of the fiercest of the Lakota warriors, and fought bravely against Custer's battalion.

Curley

One of the four Crow scouts who went with Custer, Curley remained with the troops on the battlefield longer than any of the other scouts.

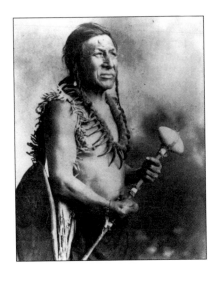

White Swan

Crow scout White Swan, along with Half Yellow Face, stayed with Reno during the Little Bighorn battle. Since they did not accompany Custer himself, they were ignored and forgotten by the press and the public.

the river. Neither Varnum nor Custer could see any trace of the camp, with or without Varnum's cheap spyglass, but the Crows swore it was there. The scouts and Varnum had also seen two small parties of Lakota on a crest of a ridge. Varnum was sure that these Indians had seen the Seventh's campfires, and would no doubt alert the village of the regiment's approach.

The new intelligence demanded another change in plans. Custer had no intention of allowing the Indians to scatter as they always did at the first sign of soldiers. If that happened, they'd be chasing the hostiles through the snow that winter. There was no choice, Custer reasoned, but to attack instantly. Soon he received news from his brother and acting aide-de-camp, Tom, that confirmed his fears of discovery.

The night before, Yates's Company F had lost a load of hardtack from a mule, and early that morning Yates had sent Sergeant William A. Curtis and two men back to find it. When they came upon the boxes a few miles to the rear, several Indians were going through them. The troopers fired upon them, and the Indians fled toward the village. Discovery by the village seemed imminent.

The sky was slightly overcast this Sunday morning, and a slight breeze made it cooler than usual as the sun rose in the sky. When the clouds burned off, the heat would be stifling. As the troopers of the Seventh broke camp, Custer briefed his officers. "The largest Indian camp on the North American continent is ahead and I am going to attack it," he told them in his high, nervous voice. The Lakota surely knew of their presence, and would soon scatter as they always did. The regiment must advance at once. There was not even time for a proper reconnaissance of the village's size or location, or the terrain surrounding it. Battle plans would have to be made on the move. He told them to detail seven men from each troop, a total of eighty-four men, to accompany the pack train, which would bring up the rear. The troops would move out immediately in order of readiness.

Boyer approached Custer as the officers walked back to their troops. He said, "General, I have been with these Indians for thirty years, and this is the largest village I have ever heard of." Custer waved him off. The strength of the enemy was the least of his worries. All he cared about was hitting the hostiles before they scattered. An army unit the size of the Seventh Cavalry could whip all the Sioux in the country—he had said it before and he still believed it.

As his men gulped down a quick breakfast and saddled up, Custer rode about the command bareback issuing orders to his officers. He paused at the Arikara cookfire. The outspoken Bloody Knife said something; Boyer interpreted for him, "He says we'll find enough Sioux to keep us fighting two or three days." Custer smiled. "I guess we'll get through with them in one day," he said.

Benteen's Company H, first to report ready, took the vanguard and led the Seventh at a walk over the divide and down to the head of a creek (later named Reno Creek) behind Custer and the scouts. The men were excited, and joked about going with Custer to the country's Centennial Exposition being held in Philadelphia—and taking the defeated Sitting Bull with them.

They halted a few minutes past noon on June 25, 1876, fifteen miles away from the Little Bighorn village. The clouds were gone and it was already warm; Custer took off his buckskin jacket and tied it onto the back of his saddle. He wore a blue-gray flannel blouse, buckskin pants tucked into high Wellington boots, and a cream-colored slouch hat turned up on the right side. A hunting knife in a beaded scabbard hung at his waist.

He divided his regiment into four battalions for flexibility since little was known of the terrain ahead, or the exact strength or precise location of the encampment. Benteen would take Companies D, H, and K totaling about 130 men on a slant to the left a few miles toward a nearby line of ridges to view the upper Little Bighorn Valley, and then rejoin the main column—Custer wanted to make absolutely sure that no Indians were on the upper Little Bighorn who could possibly endanger him from the rear. And he knew that Lakota villages often consisted of several groups of lodges stretched along the banks of a stream, as was the case at the Battle of the Washita. Captain Thomas M. McDougall and Company B would guard the pack train, commanded by Lieutenant Edward Mathey, and the 84 trooper-packers; they would start down Reno Creek twenty minutes after the others. To Reno, Custer gave Companies A, G, and M, about 150 officers and enlisted men. Custer would lead five companies of some 225 horsemen—C, E, F, I, and L. His nephew Autie and newspaperman Kellogg would ride with him. He directed Varnum and several of the scouts ahead. The Arikaras would accompany Reno and were told to steal or stampede the Lakota pony herd, since without them the hostiles could not escape.

Benteen was quick to speak up. He said, "Hadn't we better keep the regiment together, General? If this is as big a camp as they say, we'll need every man we have."

Custer only said, "You have your orders."

Benteen turned to the left and led his command southwest across low hills toward the bluffs. A few minutes later, Custer and Reno led their battalions at a fast trot side by side down opposite sides of the creek, four abreast, toward the Little Bighorn. The country around them was marked by low hills covered with sagebrush and occasional cottonwoods. On either side the ground was cut by deep ravines that fed into the creek. The troopers followed the narrow valley of the mostly dry Reno Creek for two hours as it wound northwest for several miles, then curved west. The heat was now blistering, and the horses stirred a large dust cloud up from the dry ground. Scouts galloped ahead and back with the latest intelligence, often prompting Custer to ride away a short distance to see for himself.

Captain Thomas M. McDougall
McDougall and Company B were in charge of the pack train at the Battle of the Little Bighorn.

Captain Thomas French
French accompanied Reno in the attack on the Indian village, leading M Troop.

Little Brave

One of the thirty-seven Arikara scouts that accompanied the Seventh Cavalry to the Little Bighorn, Little Brave died on the Reno skirmish line.

Goose

Arikara scout Goose, who had accompanied Custer on the Black Hills Expedition, was badly wounded while fighting alongside Reno's troops in the valley.

Three or four miles above the river, on a flat on the north side of the creek, Custer's battalion came upon the site of a large abandoned camp where a few tepees remained. The columns stopped only briefly to investigate. Inside one was a dead warrior, no doubt mortally wounded at the Battle of the Rosebud. Acting on orders from Custer, the soldiers set the tepee on fire. From a high rocky bluff opposite the tepee, the scouts had been watching a band of about forty warriors moving leisurely away from the column, apparently alerted by the cavalry's dust. They were a few miles away, and seemed to be the rear guard for the rest of the fleeing village. Custer, already concerned over the whereabouts of Benteen—it had been two hours, and he should have returned by now—was further vexed. It appeared that the camp was already beginning to break up. What everyone feared might occur was indeed happening: The Indians were scattering. Custer beckoned Reno with his hand, and Reno rode up. "You will take your battalion and try to bring them to battle and I will support you," Custer told him. "Take the scouts with you." Reno's three companies started forward at a fast trot down the creek after the fleeing Indians. Custer's depleted force followed behind at a slower pace; Custer looked to his backtrail for Benteen. The men had been riding hard for the past three days, but they had ridden harder many times. They were about to close in for the kill, and their spirits were high.

A half hour later, just minutes before 3 P.M., Reno's battalion reached a small flat a mile and a half above the river. The Crow scouts sighted two Lakota riding up the creek toward them. When the Lakota saw the column and its dust, they galloped back toward the camp, then veered north onto a ridge overlooking the river. On a ridge just above the Little Bighorn, they alerted the village by circling their horses, an Indian signal of danger.

The Little Bighorn in this part of the valley was a smallish river—not much more than a creek, actually—that looped back upon itself again and again as it meandered north down the valley. Though it was not more than two to five feet in depth, its banks, particularly the east one, were steep and soft, making it difficult to ford in most places. Its water was cool and clear. Though hills and ravines sloped down to the river's banks on the east side, along the water's western banks were occasional stands of cottonwoods. The Big Horn Mountains rose some distance to the south, and a gently rolling prairie extended a mile or two west to where flat shelflands rose a hundred feet. On this prairie, the vast Indian pony herd, now more than 12,000 strong, grazed.

The Indian village stretched almost two miles along the stream. Each lodge was in its assigned place and arranged in tribal circles, as was customary. Farthest down the river, at the northern end of the camp, were the fierce Cheyenne, led by war chiefs Two Moon, Little Horse, and White Bull. Some Arapahos camped with them. The Oglalas, under Crazy Horse, were next. Below them were the Sans Arcs, led by Spotted Eagle and Fast Bear, then the Minneconjous, whose war chiefs were Hump, Lame

Reno's Retreat
Cheyenne warrior White Bird's pictograph depicted the Indians' rout of Reno and his troops' retreat to the river.

Lieutenant Benjamin H. Hodgson

Reno's adjutant, Hodgson was killed while crossing the river during Reno's retreat from the valley.

Lieutenant Luther Rector Hare

Hare helped Varnum oversee the Indian scouts.

Deer, and Fast Bull. Next was the circle of Scabby Head's Blackfeet. The last circle to the south belonged to the Hunkpapas of Sitting Bull, whose war chiefs included Gall, Crow King, and Black Moon, all ferocious fighters. Scattered throughout the several circles were contingents of other Lakota tribes, including Two Kettle, Brule, Yanktonai, and Santee. All told there were as many as 8,000 to 10,000 Indians, with between 1,500 and 2,000 fighting men—many of them young men from the agencies, fed and armed, ironically, by the U.S. government.

The Indians had occupied this site for only a few days, having moved five miles north on June 23 after reports of large herds of antelope grazing nearby. They knew there were other cavalrymen in the next valley to the east, though the Indians sighted by Varnum and the scouts from the Crow's Nest had been Red Cloud Agency Indians on their way home. The Lakota encampment knew the "pony soldiers" were coming. They just didn't know when, though they suspected an attack on June 26 at the soonest.

Ironically, despite Custer's worries over the discovery of the regiment, they had come close to surprising the hostiles. Though a few were out hunting game, most of the warriors were still in their lodges recovering from a late night of socializing and celebrating the Rosebud victory. Women and children moved about in the early afternoon. Some of the older boys tended to the pony herd to the west. Some women attended to everyday chores while others gathered wild turnips a small distance away from camp. Hundreds of children splashed in the cool waters of the river, which was about 100 feet wide at this point. But when news of the approaching soldiers came, the alarm spread quickly. The warriors had only a few minutes' warning, but they burst from their lodges with weapons in hand. Some herded the women and children toward the far end of the village. Others ran to their ponies. The preparations for battle started a dust cloud that Custer misinterpreted as escape.

Now, only a mile or so from the river, interpreter Gerard kicked his horse up onto a little knoll next to the creek and saw the rising dust cloud and frenzied activity. He waved his hat and yelled to Custer, "Here are your Indians running like devils." Down below, Custer sent Adjutant Cooke forward to Reno with new orders: "The village is running away. Take your battalion across the river at as rapid a pace as prudent and charge afterwards. I will support you." Custer directed Captain Keogh down to the ford with Reno to assess the situation and report back.

Reno moved out immediately, following the Indian trail along the right bank at a fast trot toward the river. He reached the Little Bighorn at a natural ford ten minutes later. The battalion watered their thirsty horses and filled their canteens for a few minutes, then regrouped on the far side. In the distance, they saw an alarming sight: Instead of fleeing, the Indians at the village two miles away

White Bull
A nephew of Sitting Bull, White Bull was already a famous Minneconjou warrior at the time of the Little Bighorn battle.

Spotted Eagle
Along with Fast Bear, Spotted Eagle led the Sans Arc Lakota at the Little Bighorn.

were gathering and riding toward them. Some of the mounted warriors galloped to and fro raising screening clouds of dust. A rattled Reno immediately sent back a courier, then another one a few minutes later, to Custer with the news that the Indians were in front of him and "in full force."

Custer, still looking for Benteen on his backtrail, had followed Reno at a slower pace. His command had stopped to water their horses halfway down to the river when he received the news of the Indians' unexpected resistance. He could wait for Benteen no longer; Reno's force needed support. Here, a half mile from the river, Custer decided to follow Boyer and the remaining four Crow scouts (two had ridden with the Arikaras)—Goes Ahead, White Man Runs Him, Hairy Moccasin, and Curley—up onto a long ridge to the right (later called Reno Hill) to view the valley and village. From there he would have more information with which to formulate a plan. Some kind of flank attack would support Reno more effectively. The question was when and where to strike—the jagged terrain and bluffs that dropped straight down to the river on this side presented unforeseen problems. Still, if they could get far enough downriver, cross, and attack . . . As brave as they were, Indians did

Two Moon
Cheyenne chief Two Moon led his warriors against Reno's men in the timber.

not stand and fight, in Custer's experience, especially when attacked from two sides. They would panic and run, as they always had, or surrender. The day would belong to the cavalry. The glory of the last great Indian battle would be the Seventh's—and Custer's.

Across the river, Reno's three companies fast-trotted side by side in columns of fours down the valley floor toward the camp, kicking up a thick cloud of dust as they advanced. Varnum and most of the white and Indian scouts rode on the left flank. The pace picked up, and as the battalion, now in full gallop, wheeled around a wooded bend in the river, a worried Reno looked over his shoulder for Custer. The heavy-drinking Reno had just swigged some whiskey to fortify himself, for he was leading troops into an engagement with Indians for the first time. His CO and his support were nowhere to be seen. A half mile ahead was a swarming mass of angry Indians moving up the valley toward them, ready and willing to defend everything dear to them— their women and children, their lives, their homeland, their freedom, and their way of life. It would be suicidal, Reno thought, to proceed.

He raised his hand and shouted a halt, then ordered his men to dismount and form a skirmish line out into the valley, several hundred yards toward the bluffs that rose 1,000 yards west of the line's end. They would fight on foot, at five-yard intervals. As the command came to a stop, an unfortunate trooper's horse bolted with him forward into the Indian ranks. He was never seen again. The battalion dismounted. Every fourth man held the reins and led the mounts to the rear and then along the right flank into the cottonwoods near the river. The remaining troopers began firing their carbines at the advancing Indians, still hundreds of yards away. The inexperienced troopers wasted ammunition by firing too quickly and haphazardly, and some of their carbines

Sitting Bull
Sitting Bull remained near the Indian camp to rally the young braves and direct the women and children to safety.

overheated and jammed—a common defect of the Springfield after a few quick rounds and one that required a trooper to scrape out the soft copper cartridge with a knife. Some of the mounted warriors turned the left flank of the thin line. The Arikaras there, directed to scatter the vast pony herd, were no match for the Cheyenne and Lakota; several Rees succeeded early on in capturing a herd of about 200 ponies but were chased back across the river by Lakota. Of the rest, a few stayed with Reno's battalion, but after three were killed and two injured, the remainder fled the field and didn't stop until they reached the supply camp at the mouth of the Powder two days later. The hostiles galloped into the rear of Reno's line. Other warriors made their way through the woods on the right, and some climbed the bluffs on the opposite side of the river to train their rifles on the troopers. Far behind them, on the high bluffs back from the river, elements of Custer's command could be seen by Reno's men, and Custer himself could be plainly seen waving his hat.

A storm of arrows began raining down on Reno's troopers. From a ravine several hundred yards toward the village, more warriors emerged. Within minutes it was clear that the position was fast becoming untenable. Reno ordered his men to withdraw into the timber that skirted the river on his right flank. The last of the troopers on the left, M Troop led by the steely Captain Thomas French, sprinted for cover into the woods. No more than fifteen minutes had passed since Reno's order to dismount.

Once in the trees, the soldiers turned and began firing into the oncoming warriors. Here an old river bank created a convenient breastwork, but the thick woods prevented an organized defense. Rifle fire from both sides was fierce—"lead was coming so fast it was knocking the dust in our eyes," remembered a trooper. The Indians were everywhere, and they were increasingly daring—they were working their way closer and closer, both from the valley side and through the river timber. Waves of warriors led by Two Moon, One Bull, and others, including Crazy Horse—who was late in arriving—crashed into the timber and fell back. Within thirty minutes the position was almost completely surrounded. Although only one or two men had been killed to this point, Reno decided that this position too was indefensible. Besides, ammunition was getting low; his fresh troopers, many of whom had never been in battle before, had exercised little fire control in the valley or in the timber. In a small clearing, Reno jumped onto his horse and ordered his men to mount. Seconds later a bullet smashed into the head of Bloody Knife, on his horse next to Reno, and the dead scout's blood and brains splattered Reno's face and uniform. The

John Grass
Grass was the chief of the Blackfeet at the Little Bighorn.

One Bull
One Bull was one of the Minneconjou leaders of the attack on Reno at the Little Bighorn.

Right: Crow King
One of Sitting Bull's Hunkpapa war chiefs, he led some eighty warriors against Custer's men on Finley Ridge and Calhoun Hill.

Below: Hump
The Minneconjou Hump (shown here with two of his wives) was badly wounded in the attack against Calhoun Hill.

flustered major called for a dismount, then ordered a mount again, and galloped from the trees. "What damn fool move is this?" yelled interpreter Gerard to Reynolds when he heard Captain Moylan repeat the command to retreat.

Reno emerged from the grove and signaled a retreat back up the valley. If his troopers could cross the river back at the ford and establish a position on the bluffs above, they could make a stand and perhaps reunite with Custer and Benteen. Reno's confused command, some still on horseback and some not, straggled after him onto the prairie. War whoops, the roar of hundreds of rifles, and thick clouds of dust surrounded them. Seventeen soldiers who never heard the command over the roar of battle remained in the woods and returned fire.

Reno led the ragged retreat (which he would later insist was a charge) out of the cottonwoods, and neglected to organize any kind of rear-guard defensive fire. Mounted Indians howling "like incarnate fiends" pressured them with rifle fire—much of it from modern single-action Henry and Winchester repeaters—and soon they were galloping alongside the troopers, slashing at them with lances and tomahawks, shooting arrows point blank, knocking them down with war clubs. Many warriors later likened it to a buffalo hunt. "The Indians picked off the troops at will," remembered Gerard later. "It was a rout, not a charge." Charley Reynolds was killed on the way to the river, pinned under his dead horse. The half-breed Lieutenant Donald McIntosh died not far away, attacked by a mob of more than fifty warriors. Isaiah Dorman's horse was downed right after he shot an Indian in the heart. On one knee, he continued to fire carefully at the Indians. He was made to die slowly and painfully, his legs below the knees shot full of bullets, then mutilated by women, who pounded him with stone hammers.

Through a thick cloud of dust the Indians drove the disorganized troopers toward the river and down its steep banks into the water. Lieutenant Varnum raced to the front of the column and attempted to stop them. "For God's sake, men, don't run; we've got to go back and save the wounded." No one paid him any attention. At the riverbank, six to eight feet above the water, they hesitated, then soldiers and horses hurled themselves into the saddle-deep Little Bighorn. The Indians reined in at the river's edge, and warriors on both banks let loose a ferocious fire into the struggling troopers below. On the far side the survivors somehow scrambled up the sheer bank to the high ground above to flop onto the ground in exhaustion. As a few officers directed skirmish operations, the agitated Reno tied a white handkerchief around his head (he had lost his hat in the retreat), then began uselessly firing his pistol at Indians a thousand yards away. Twenty-nine men died and ten more were wounded in the chaotic flight to the river and across it. "The crossing was not covered," remembered Lieutenant Luther Rector Hare. "If the Indians had followed us in force to the hill-top, they would have got us all."

But a curious thing happened. As Reno and his men regrouped on the knoll, the warriors seemed suddenly to lose interest. Most of them turned their horses around and galloped downstream with a vengeance.

Short Bull
Brother of He Dog and nephew of the great Oglala leader Red Cloud, Short Bull helped drive Reno and his men out of the valley and into the hills.

Kicking Bear
A nephew of Sitting Bull, the Oglala Kicking Bear was involved in the attack among Reno's men leaving the timber. He later became heavily involved in the Ghost Dance upheaval of 1890.

Low Dog
The Oglala Low Dog was part of the attack against Custer's battalion.

Wooden Leg
The Northern Cheyenne Wooden Leg was part of the Indian group that attacked Reno's troops as they retreated toward the river.

Fool Bull
In this photograph from 1900, Lakota medicine man Fool Bull holds the buffalo-hide shield which he carried into the Battle of the Little Bighorn.

White Man Runs Him
White Man Runs Him was a Crow scout who accompanied Custer at the Little Bighorn.

Far left: ## He Dog
Oglala leader He Dog killed some of the Indian scouts during Reno's retreat to the river.

Left: ## Spotted Elk
The Minneconjou chief Spotted Elk fought Reno in the valley, then rode against Custer.

Lakota Warriors

A group of Lakota warriors participate in a celebratory grass dance on the reservation at Fort Yates, Dakota Territory.

Right: **Tall Bull**

A Northern Cheyenne, Tall Bull followed Lame White Man's charge up the hill against Custer's men.

Far right: **Brave Wolf**

The Northern Cheyenne war chief Brave Wolf fought against Reno in the valley and then galloped north to fight against Custer.

Left: **Gall**
The war chief of the Hunkpapas, Gall fought at the Little Bighorn with only a hatchet. Two of his wives and three children were killed by Reno's men early in the battle, and he crossed the river and fought for revenge against the troopers on Calhoun Hill.

Below left: **American Horse**
A Northern Cheyenne chief, American Horse attacked Reno's men as they retreated from the timber, then fought against Yates's men at the ford.

Below, center: **Flying By**
The Minneconjou Flying By had his horse shot from under him as he galloped against Reno's men during the retreat from the river.

Below right: **Flying Hawk**
The Oglala Flying Hawk, another of Sitting Bull's nephews, followed Crazy Horse against Reno's men as they galloped out of the timber. He then followed Crazy Horse across the river, up Deep Coulee, and down Battle Ridge after Custer's men.

Dusty Hill

*"We will all be cleaned out . . .
we have no chance at all."*
—Scout Mitch Boyer

Custer and his five companies had followed Boyer and the Indians up onto a ridge (Reno Hill) overlooking the lower end of the valley. From there they saw Reno charging down the valley toward the village. It was their first clear view of the Indian camp, and it was every bit as large as they had been told. Some of the horses became so excited that their riders were hard put to hold them in ranks. "Hold your horses in, boys," said Custer. "There are plenty of them down there for all of us." A half-mile or so past Reno Hill, he signaled a halt and galloped up onto a high hill (Sharpshooter Ridge) to assess the situation. Then he waved his hat to the men below at the base of the hill and said, "Courage, boys, we've got them. As soon as we get through, we will go back to our

Call of the Bugle
Custer's Seventh Cavalry prepared to make its last stand in artist J. K. Ralston's painting.

station." Almost every man doffed his hat and cheered. Thirty-nine days had passed since Custer had seen Libbie. It would be good to get back to Fort Lincoln.

He conferred with his officers and scouts, and they passed field glasses around. Down in the valley, Reno's men were dismounting and forming a skirmish line well short of the village. Confronting them were fifty or so warriors. Why had Reno stopped? Custer likely wondered. No matter; Reno should be able to hold his position for a while—long enough for Custer to strike. In the village, at least the portion they could see, only children, women, dogs, and ponies were visible. Where were the rest of the warriors? In their tents asleep? Someone suggested they might be buffalo hunting. Either way, it was a golden opportunity to capture the village without much of a fight and use the families as hostages. If they could seize the women and children, the warriors would have no choice but to surrender. But where was Benteen? Three hours had passed since he had left on the scouting assignment that should have taken no more than half that time.

A few minutes later Tom Custer broke away and trotted back to his own C Troop. Relaying orders from his brother, he sent Sergeant Daniel Kanipe back to McDougall and Benteen with word of the big village and calling for the pack train to come straight across country instead of following the regiment's trail. If any packs except those with ammunition became loose, they were to cut them away and continue on quickly. "And if you see Benteen tell him to come on quick—a big Indian camp," he concluded. Kanipe turned his horse and left.

It was time to move. The immediate flank attack Custer had planned was out of the question as the bluffs here were too steep to approach the river. They would continue north to find a good ford. Custer led his men down into a ravine (Cedar Coulee) that curved at a northeast angle away from the river. At a bend a half mile later, Custer halted the command. He released the Crows from duty, since they had not been hired to fight. Boyer elected to stay, as did Curley. The other three Crows turned south and galloped away. Custer, Boyer, Curley, and a few officers spurred their horses up onto a close-by hill to observe developments. The situation had changed dramatically in fifteen minutes' time. From the ridge they could see across the river to the dusty valley. Reno's skirmish line was fast deteriorating, with hundreds of Indians attacking and outflanking them, and more organizing at the now-bustling camp. Even as they watched, Reno was pulling his men into the timber. He should be able to make a stand there, it appeared, but he would soon need help in the form of reinforcements and ammunition. Boyer pointed out a large gully below (Medicine Tail Coulee) that led to the river across from what looked to be the center of the village.

They rejoined the command in Cedar Coulee. Custer called for

"Courage, boys, we've got them. As soon as we get through, we will go back to our station."
—Custer to his cavalrymen after sighting the Little Bighorn encampment

Lieutenant Tom Custer

Tom Custer was his brother's acting aide-de-camp during their final campaign. His body was mutilated almost beyond recognition at the Little Bighorn.

Custer
The last photo of Custer ever taken, late April 1876.

trumpeter John Martin, his orderly that day, and told him to take a message as fast as he could to Benteen. Adjutant Cooke, fearful that the young Italian immigrant—Giovanni Martini was his real name— might flummox the important message, scribbled it onto a small piece of paper and handed it to Martin: "Benteen: Come on. Big Village. Be quick. Bring Packs. W. W. Cooke. P.S. Bring Pacs."

Martin turned and galloped back the way they'd come. His last sight of the command was his fellow troopers moving away down the ravine. Ten minutes later, as he left Cedar Coulee, he met Boston Custer riding from the pack train toward him. "Where's the General?" yelled Boston. "Right behind the next ridge," replied Martin, then warned him that there were a great number of Indians. "I am going to join the command anyhow," Boston said, then lashed his horse forward in pursuit of his brothers.

Boston caught up to the command at the junction of Cedar Coulee and Medicine Tail Coulee, where the troops were briefly

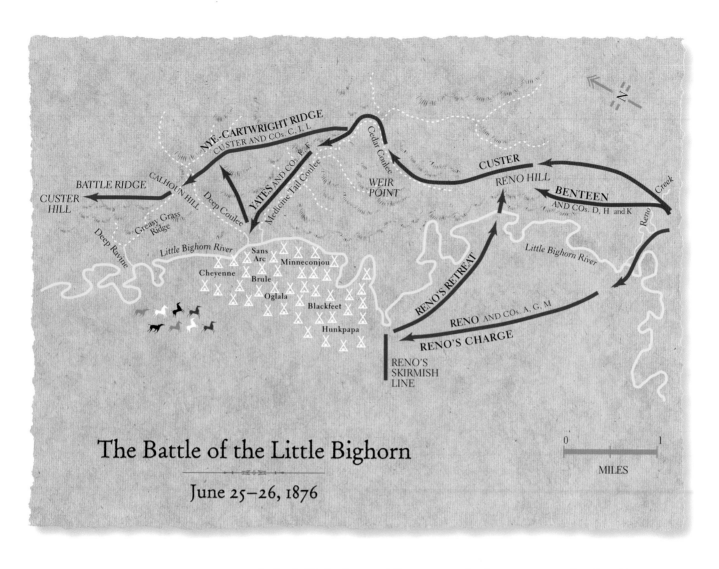

The Battle of the Little Bighorn

June 25–26, 1876

halted. He had passed Benteen at the lone tepee, so he shouldn't be too far behind, he told Armstrong. The command resumed its march down the gully. Up on Weir Peak, Boyer and Curley witnessed Reno's retreat from the timber and the panicked river crossing, and they rode down to tell Custer of it. Less than half a mile down the coulee Custer halted the command again.

What to do? Attack immediately, to support Reno's precarious position, or wait for Benteen's reinforcements and ammunition? From a high bluff (East Ridge), Custer decided to send Companies E and F under Captain Yates down Medicine Tail Coulee toward the village. Yates would feint a charge across the river and into the camp. The threat toward the women and children there would surely draw off the warriors pursuing Reno and buy time—maybe enough for a full-strength attack. Custer instructed the buglers to blast a call to accompany Yates and perhaps throw a scare into the enemy. With Companies C, I, and L under Captain Keogh, Custer proceeded northwest over the north rim of Medicine Tail Coulee to keep in sight as much as possible. Two miles to the south he could see a large dust cloud—what could only be Benteen's command reaching

Reno's position atop Reno Hill. Surely they would regroup and follow the Indians north toward Custer; then they could trap the Indians in a makeshift pincers movement.

Upriver, where Reno's tattered command had taken cover on Reno Hill, word began circulating among the Indians. More troops—Yates's feint—were moving to attack the lower village. The warriors left Reno's shell-shocked force and rode down the valley.

At 4:15 P.M. as the sun seared high in a cloudless sky, Yates's battalion trotted down the ravine. A quarter mile from the river, the detachment dismounted and began shooting into a handful of Cheyenne on foot between them and the river. After a few minutes of light firing during which two troopers were killed, a loud volley from Keogh's battalion signaled them to leave. Yates's men mounted and moved downriver, climbing back up the bluffs in columns of fours.

As soon as the cavalry left the ford, hundreds of Indians swarmed across the river, some on horses, others on foot. They crawled up ravines on both sides of Yates's command as the soldiers rode toward the re-union point. The troopers moved slowly uphill in an orderly fashion, fighting

Trumpeter John Martin

Martin, an Italian immigrant, was the last white man to see Custer alive.

Custer's Note

Custer sent trumpeter John Martin to take this last note to Captain Frederick Benteen, urging him to hurry and bring supplies. Benteen later rewrote the orders legibly at the top.

Adjutant William W. Cooke

Cooke sporting his formidable Dundreary whiskers. The Canadian-born adjutant was the fastest runner and the best shot in the regiment.

Captain George W. Yates

Yates was a dependable soldier who had served with Custer in the Civil War.

bravely, but some of the horses, unused to battle in general and Indian fighting in particular, reared up and threw their riders. Several more troopers were cut down.

Most of Yates's detachment reunited with Custer and Keogh's battalion atop a ridge (Nye-Cartwright Ridge) almost a mile northeast from the ford. There, Custer surveyed the scene while his men fired down into the hundreds of warriors advancing on his position. Most of the Indians had abandoned their ponies to creep up the gullies on foot. Others were streaming toward the troopers from the south, the west, and now up the ravine below them (Deep Coulee). There was only one choice open to Custer: Move north, to keep the bulk of the enemy between him and the rest of the command under Reno and Benteen. They would surely be along soon.

Mitch Boyer, injured and without a horse, had been talking with Custer and his brother Tom. He walked over to Curley. "You had better leave now, for we will all be cleaned out," he said—it was time for Curley to save himself. Curley insisted that Boyer also go. Boyer cut him off. He was too badly wounded, he said. He would stay and fight it out, though he believed they all would be killed. "Curley, you are very young and do not know very much about fighting. I advise you to leave us, and if you can get away by detouring and keeping out of the way of the Sioux, do so, and go to the other soldiers [Terry's men] and tell them that all are killed. That man," he said, pointing to Custer, "will stop at nothing . . . we have no chance at all." They shook hands, and Curley turned east and galloped away. He soon rode down into a ravine and out of sight.

Custer led his men off the hill into Deep Coulee, then up onto a hogback ridge (Calhoun Hill) set back from the river that continued north for more than a mile. Custer quickly deployed Keogh's three companies along the ridge—L first, then C, and I farther north. The troopers dismounted and formed a skirmish line. Custer, at the head of Yates's two companies, continued north along the line of ridges, searching for a high, flat spot to make a stand on. The uneven terrain was a bad place for cavalry to fight—the broken ground was full of ravines and gullies, the ridges were low and offered no defensible position. If they could find a place to regroup, his seven other troops would march to the sound of the gunfire and the thundering volleys of rifle fire they must have heard. More and more Indians were at their heels and on their flanks, sending a steady barrage of arrows and bullets into their midst. There had been little close action yet—most of the firing had been at a distance, with few results. But there seemed to be no end of warriors following them on both flanks, slowly closing in on the troopers.

At first the warriors kept at a distance, using for cover the many gullies, hollows, small knolls, and clumps of sagebrush, only jumping up for an instant to fire their rifles at the enemies on the ridge above. Many loosed high, arcing volleys of arrows that rained down

Left: **Lame White Man**
The Cheyenne chief Lame White Man (sitting next to Wild Hog in this 1873 photo) led a heroic charge up Custer Hill against Company E. He was shot dead near the top of the ridge.

Below: **Lieutenant Algernon E. "Fresh" Smith**
Smith was an able officer who displayed conspicuous bravery during the Civil War.

onto horses and men. Then the Indians charged Keogh's dismounted battalion, part of which now extended down a ridge (Finley Ridge) toward the river. They were repulsed by fire from the troopers. But more warriors, hundreds more, most of them now on foot, were surrounding the bluecoats. Others galloped up Deep Coulee to attack the cavalry's eastern flank. Still more stormed across the river and ran across the wide Greasy Grass Ridge that gently sloped up from the water. More than a thousand warriors were now approaching the 200-odd men of Custer's command, their ululating death-wails and shrill war yells everywhere around the terrified soldiers. Crazy Horse galloped up to and past the soldiers to draw and waste the soldiers' single-shot rifle fire, after which the inspired Indians quickly charged their lines with reduced risk. They soon cut off Custer's squadron, which was still riding north, from Keogh's detachment.

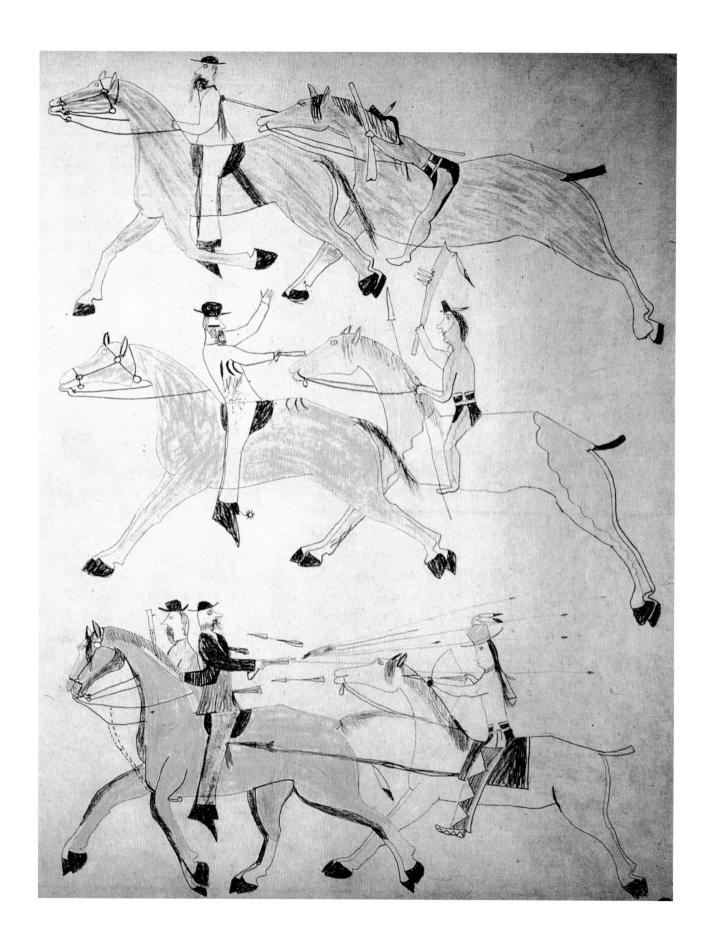

Along the high ground of Calhoun Ridge, Lieutenants Calhoun and Crittenden of Company L put up a valiant fight. They held their positions with their men until they were overwhelmed by warriors. Keogh led the remainder of his men north after Custer, and made a stand on a ridge (Battle Ridge) a few hundred yards away. Rifle fire from warriors on hills far to the south and east picked off his troopers. Then Crazy Horse and Two Moon led their braves up and over the ridge from the east and swarmed into the troopers in a charge that broke Keogh's line. From the south, Gall led his whooping men in a rush into the troopers' rear. The remaining soldiers, some on foot, some on horses, turned and broke toward Custer along the ridge, but only a few escaped. The men on Finley Ridge, cut off from their brothers, broke downhill for the river, but none made it far. The ground on Calhoun Ridge was soon littered with bodies. No one in a blue uniform remained standing.

One trooper escaped around the Indians and galloped north, away from the battle. Several warriors took off after him. He managed to ride a long way. His pursuers were about to give up when they saw him take his pistol and shoot himself. Other troopers also turned their pistols on themselves when it was clear there was no help—"Keep the last bullet for yourself" was a phrase that many soldiers in Indian country, fearful of torture and mutilation while still alive, took to heart.

Toward the northern end of the long ridge, Custer halted his depleted command and looked around through the thick smoke and dust. He now had less than two companies with him around his headquarters banner. The number of wounded, which Dr. George E. Lord was now tending to on the ground, was mounting. The pressure on them from behind and on both flanks was relentless. Yelling warriors were making their way up the gently sloping Greasy Grass Ridge toward them from the river, using the broken terrain effectively as cover. Hundreds more were encroaching from the rear up the northeast face of the ridge that the general and his men now occupied (Custer Hill). Panicked cavalry mounts galloped this way and that through the chaos as the sun dropped toward the low hills in the west.

The rearguard action had only held for a short time. It was time to make a stand. If they could hold out until the rest of the Seventh showed up, they could still win the day. Glory was still theirs for the taking if Custer's Luck still held—and it would be even sweeter against such a strong opponent. Custer had never seen Indians fight like this, so fearless, so persistently aggressive, so confident, so organized.

Facing page: **Chasing Custer's Cavalry**
A detail from one of the pictographs painted by Red Horse showing the Indians chasing down wounded cavalrymen.

Lieutenant William Van Wyck Reily
Newly commissioned, Reily joined the Seventh Cavalry in May 1875, just before the regiment left Fort Lincoln. He was still learning to ride a horse when he was killed at the Little Bighorn.

Captain Frederick W. Benteen
Benteen was the de facto leader and the undisputed hero of the Reno Hill siege.

Lieutenant George D. Wallace

Wallace was the acting engineer officer and official itinerist of the campaign. He rode with Reno's battalion.

Lieutenant Winfield Scott Edgerly

Edgerly was second-in-command of Troop D.

There was not enough room below the crest of the ridge for the hundred men he had left. Southwest, from the river a half mile away, Indians were approaching up a large gully (Deep Ravine) toward the command. Above the roar of screams, gunfire, and pounding horse hooves, Custer yelled at Lieutenant Smith to take E Troop down against the Indians, then form a skirmish line along the slight divide above the ravine. That would buy some time and hold the Indians away from the wounded. Smith rode downhill with his men, all mounted on gray steeds.

When the troopers charged, the Indians retreated and scattered downhill. But as the troopers pulled back and dismounted along the ridge above the ravine, hundreds of warriors worked their way back up the gullies, goaded by an older Cheyenne chief named Lame White Man. In the first rush uphill, Lame White Man fell dead with several others, but soon they had the soldiers almost completely surrounded. Inspired by the maniacal charges of the Suicide Boys—a group of about twenty young men who had taken a vow to fight to the death—the screaming warriors closed in for hand-to-hand fighting. Some were bold enough to count coup on living enemies, touching them with their coup sticks. The troopers fired their guns as fast as they could load them and killed many Indians, but soon E Company was destroyed. A few cavalrymen with horses escaped to rejoin Custer, Lieutenant Smith among them, but the rest died along the ridge as the Indians rushed upon the bluecoats with spears, clubs, hatchets, and guns. As they overwhelmed the men of E Troop, the Indians grabbed the guns and cartridges of the dead soldiers. Many of the horses stampeded down to the river, where they stopped and drank. The Indians turned their full attention to the hill above.

Near the crest, Custer stood, surrounded by the last of his men. Most were sitting or lying prone, their hats off, as they trained their rifles on the hundreds of Indians crawling toward them. The dense dust and gunsmoke choked them, and the stealth and relentlessness of the enemy was terrifying. Many of the general's favorites were there: Tom was still with him, and Boston, who had galloped full speed from the pack train to be with his brothers; Custer's nephew, Autie, crouched on the ground behind a dead horse; his adjutant, Cooke; Captain Yates; Lieutenant William Van Wyck Reily; and Boyer, the best scout on the frontier. Isolated troopers staggered into their position from the south and west, the last remnants of Keogh's battalion. Fifty men surrounded Custer, many of them wounded, most of them exhausted, coughing and gasping for breath.

There were perhaps thirty horses left. Custer ordered several of them moved into a large, rough semicircle around the command, to be shot and used as breastworks. From behind the dead mounts, the general and his men continued to fire into the approaching warriors, now even closer on all sides and pouring hundreds of rounds into them every minute. Arrows rained down among them like hail.

Custer's Last Fight
This illustration by A. R. Waud was one of the earliest and most accurate depictions of Custer's Last Stand.

Far left: **Dr. Henry R. Porter**
Porter treated the wounded on Reno Hill.

Left: **Lieutenant Camillus L. "Charles" DeRudio**
The Italian DeRudio had barely escaped execution for his part in a plot to kill Napoleon III. He immigrated to the United States and saw action in the last days of the Civil War.

Custer's Last Charge
A fanciful Currier & Ives litho-graph printed in 1876.

Though they were putting up a ferocious firefight, his men were dying more quickly now. Custer threw down his Remington Creedmore rifle and pulled out his two English Webley Bulldog pistols. It would be close action from here on in.

A few troopers on the last of the horses took off along the ridge in a desperate attempt to escape. None succeeded. Another group of about thirty soldiers jumped up and ran down the slope toward the river. Soon they were surrounded and overwhelmed by Indians with arrows, clubs, and hatchets. Not one made it to the stream.

Indians on horses swirled around the knoll, pumping shots into the last of the cavalrymen as fast as they could. Soon only a few soldiers were left. There was no hope of rescue, they knew now. Custer was one of the last to die, firing his pistols at warriors so close he could see into their eyes. A bullet hit him in his left side and another pierced his left temple, killing him instantly.

Four miles south, the remains of Reno's broken command had scrambled through a relentless hail of bullets up the steep riverbank to the bluffs above. Then the Indians had turned and rode north, down both sides of the Little Bighorn. Only a few remained, some on the high bluffs downstream and others in the underbrush along the river. As the exhausted, demoralized troopers, some of them sobbing openly, gathered their wits, they spied Benteen's command approaching from the south.

Benteen was peeved that he had been given such an inglorious task while others would be in at the kill. He had slowly marched some five miles southwest over several ridges, far enough to satisfy him that there were no Indians in that part of the Little Bighorn Valley. He then turned right and headed northwest down a narrow valley, hitting the battalion's trail near Reno Creek. A mile later, he watered the horses at a morass in the creek bed for twenty minutes while some of his subordinates muttered about the lengthy delay. About a mile down the trail, Kanipe galloped up and delivered his message about the pack train, then added, "They want you up there as quick as you can get there—they have struck a big Indian camp." Benteen picked up the pace a bit and soon encountered trumpeter Martin with his even more urgent message. They continued on. Soon gunfire could be heard ahead of them. Benteen ordered his

Dead Cavalrymen
Red Horse's pictograph showing the Seventh Cavalry dead.

Victorious

A detail from one of Red Horse's pictograph paintings showing the victorious Indians leaving the battleground.

snipers remained to fire into the cavalrymen now and then throughout the night.

The 350-odd soldiers spent most of the night of June 25–26 digging pits in the porous soil; there were only three or four spades, so the men used tin cups, knives, spoons, and fingers. Some of the exhausted men fell asleep as they worked. While Reno proceeded to get drunk, Benteen deployed the men in an effective perimeter defense, erecting what little barricades were available, and Dr. Henry R. Porter cared for the wounded in the center of the swale. That night, thirteen men who had been left behind in the timber during Reno's retreat sneaked into camp. The main topic of conversation was the fate or location of Custer's command. The consensus was that what was left of his battalion was holed up just as they were, somewhere downstream. Some troopers wondered if Custer had continued north to join Terry's column. At some point that night, Reno approached Benteen with a plan: "I propose to mount all my men that can ride on horses and mules, and destroy the property that we cannot take with us, and make a retreat to the wagon train at the mouth of the Powder River." Benteen looked at him. "What are you going to do with the wounded that cannot ride?" he asked. Reno said, "We will have to abandon them." The shocked Benteen said forcibly, "You can't do that." It was never mentioned again.

On the morning of June 26, the Indians attacked just after first light. The soldiers were better entrenched, and they returned fire when possible. But throughout the morning the Indian fire was relentless, especially from the higher ridges to the east and north. Many of the horses and mules in the center of the depression were killed. At one point the warriors came close and massed for an attack, but Benteen led his men in a charge that routed them. Later, he persuaded Reno to order a full-force counterattack out beyond the perimeter that drove back the encroaching Indians. Throughout the day, Benteen was magnificent, walking blithely about the position in plain sight and disregarding the bullets whizzing around him, reassuring and inspiring the men: "This is a groundhog case, men. It

Seventh Cavalry Guidon
This blood-stained guidon of the Seventh Cavalry was found under the body of a dead trooper after the Battle of the Little Bighorn.

Comanche

Myles Keogh's horse, Comanche, was the only survivor found on the field of the Custer fight. He was treated as a hero and retired with honor.

General Alfred Terry brought the terrible news: Every man of the five companies under Custer's command had been found dead four miles downstream—a total of 210 men.

is live or die. We must fight it out." Reno, on the other hand, spent most of the day hiding in his rifle pit.

Morning clouds had burned off and the heat was unbearable. The lack of water was a serious problem, especially for the wounded. While four sharpshooters (coincidentally all German boys) stood up to draw the Indian fire and threw as much lead as they could into the enemy, volunteers crept down a ravine and ran thirty feet in plain sight of Indian shooters to the river to fill canteens and pots with water. One man was killed and another wounded in the leg, which would be amputated that night. For their bravery, fifteen water carriers and the four sharpshooters would later receive the Medal of Honor.

After noon, the fusillade slowed down and soon virtually disappeared, save for an occasional shot. The Indians set fire to the prairie grass in the valley, and a thick cloud of smoke soon covered it. A few hours before sunset, the smoke lifted. The soldiers on the bluffs stood and watched in awe as nearly 10,000 Indian men, women, and children, on foot and horseback, with their pony herd, travois, and dogs, slowly proceeded south up the west side of the valley toward the Big Horn Mountains—"like some Biblical exodus," remembered trooper Charles Windolph. Behind them was a mass of debris, the remains of one of the largest known gathering of Plains Indians on the North American continent.

The soldiers were relieved but wary—the Indians might only be moving their families to safety before renewing their attack. They spent the rest of the day watering their horses and themselves, and during the night buried their dead and moved to a position closer to the river and farther from the stench of the dead horses. Four more men made their way into camp, among them Lieutenant Camillus L. "Charles" DeRudio, the Italian count's son who was sentenced to life imprisonment on Devil's Island for his part in an assassination attempt on Emperor Napoleon III. He had escaped with twelve other prisoners in a hollow log, and later immigrated to the United States and served in the Union army.

On the morning of June 27, the soldiers cheered as Terry's men approached up the valley from the north. Terry brought the terrible news: Every man of the five companies under Custer's command had been found dead four miles downstream—a total of 210 men. Combined with Reno's 53 dead and 60 wounded, half the Seventh Cavalry had been killed or incapacitated.

The following day, June 28, 1876, Reno's men buried the dead on and around Battle Ridge. Most of the corpses had been stripped, scalped, and mutilated—a common Indian custom, the aim of which was to hinder the dead man's activities in the afterlife. The bodies were swollen and discolored after two days in the hot sun, and clouds of flies were everywhere. Greenback dollars fluttered about the battlefield. Dead horses lay here and there; only one or two were Indian mounts. Broken knife blades lying near the dead troopers confirmed that several carbines had jammed during the fight. Just below the crest of Custer Hill lay the bodies of Custer and about fifty others, including many of his officers. Custer's body was untouched except for a bullet hole in his left breast, another in his left temple, and a gash in his right thigh, which is how Lakota warriors marked slain enemies. Not far away was Tom Custer, his skull crushed flat, his body mutilated beyond recognition and bristling with arrows. Only a tattoo on his arm identified him.

The shocked troopers quickly buried their brother soldiers, scooping out shallow graves and barely covering the bodies with a little dirt and sagebrush. The officers received slightly better treatment: deeper graves and markers for future identification. Three missing officers, Lieutenants James Ezekiel Porter, Henry M. Harrington, and James Garland Sturgis, were never identified.

A few badly wounded cavalry mounts wandered among the carnage. They were all destroyed except one: Comanche, Captain Keogh's bay, whose seven wounds were bound up. He would recover to live another fifteen years, the pride of the Seventh Cavalry. In 1878, a general order would decree that Comanche would never be ridden again.

On the morning of June 30, Reno's sixty wounded men were carried aboard the *Far West*; Captain Marsh had guided his steamer all the way up the Big Horn to the mouth of the Little Bighorn. A few days later he piloted his boat down the Yellowstone and the Missouri in record time, docking at Bismarck late on July 5. The *Far West*'s speed record on the Missouri of 710 miles in fifty-four hours would never be topped. After briefing the telegraph operator on the news, Marsh took his boat down to Fort Lincoln and moved the wounded ashore into the post hospital.

Just before dawn on the cool, clear morning of July 6, officers went house to house at Fort Lincoln and broke the bad news to the Seventh's new widows and orphans. Libbie Custer was the first told. After recovering from the initial shock, she pulled a shawl over her shoulders and accompanied the officers to inform the other twenty-three wives whose men had died on the Little Bighorn.

Above: **The *Far West***
The steamer brought supplies to the cavalry, and then brought back the bodies of those killed at the Little Bighorn.

Below: **Captain Grant Marsh**
Marsh was the pilot of the Far West.

Chapter 9

Aftermath

"I regard Custer's massacre as a sacrifice of troops brought on by Custer himself, that was wholly unnecessary— wholly unnecessary."
—President Ulysses S. Grant

The full story of Custer's defeat reached the East on the morning of July 6, while the country was still celebrating its centennial. The death of the country's best-known Indian fighter and 260 men of the illustrious Seventh Cavalry—at the hands of undisciplined savages, no less—stunned the nation. How did it happen? Americans asked, and why?

Everyone had an opinion. The *New York Herald* asked "Who Slew Custer?" and supplied the answer: "The celebrated peace policy of General Grant, which feeds, clothes and takes care of their noncombatant force while the men are killing our troops—that is what killed Custer." The *Chicago Tribune* disagreed: "Custer preferred to make a reckless dash and take

Crow Scouts
Custer's four Crow Indian scouts gathered together in 1913 at the gravemarkers on Custer Hill. From left, White Man Runs Him, Hairy Moccasin, Curley, and Goes Ahead.

General Philip H. Sheridan
Sheridan commanded the Division of the Missouri in the 1870s.

General William Tecumseh Sherman
Sherman was general-in-chief of the U.S. Army in the 1870s.

the consequences, in the hope of making a personal victory . . . rather than wait for a sufficiently powerful force to make the fight successful and share the glory with others." Most active army officers agreed. One of the few to defend Custer was his friend, Colonel Nelson Miles, who years later pointed out that no commander can win "with seven-twelfths of the command remaining out of the engagement when within sound of his rifle shots."

Then began the inevitable game of placing blame and pointing fingers, and the predictable avoidance of responsibility. President Grant stated publicly, "I regard Custer's massacre as a sacrifice of troops brought on by Custer himself, that was wholly unnecessary—wholly unnecessary." Lieutenant General Philip Sheridan also blamed Custer, though he softened his approach; the fault, he said, was not due to a "recklessness or want of judgment, but to a misapprehension of the situation and to a superabundance of courage." General Terry, for his part, insisted that his orders had been disobeyed, though his first report, written on June 27, made no mention of his plan of a coordinated attack involving Custer and Gibbon. In his second report, a confidential one leaked to the *Philadelphia Inquirer* and published on July 7, he discussed his plan to "bring the infantry into action . . . I desired to make sure of things by getting up every available man."

There were some who spoke up in Custer's defense. Two days after the headlines, his old friend and one-time enemy, Tom Rosser, wrote a letter published in the *St. Paul Pioneer Press*: "I feel that Custer would have succeeded had Reno, with all the reserve of seven companies, passed through and joined Custer after the first repulse . . . As a soldier I would sooner today lie in the grave of Gen. Custer and his gallant comrades alone in that distant wilderness, that when the 'last trumpet' sounds I could rise to judgment from my post of duty, than to live in the place of the survivors of the siege in the hills."

The quest for a scapegoat led to Major Reno, Custer's second-in-command. Less than six months after the battle, Custer's first biographer, Frederick Whittaker, published *A Complete Life of Gen. George A. Custer*. In it, he praised Custer and accused Reno of cowardice in failing to hasten to Custer's assistance, and he called for a military investigation. In May 1878, Whittaker wrote an impassioned letter to Congress urging an investigation. The continuing criticism prompted Reno to request an official inquiry to clear his name.

In Chicago on January 13, 1879, the Reno Court of Inquiry convened for almost a month to hear the testimony of twenty-three witnesses, including most of the Seventh's surviving officers, a few enlisted men, and some civilian participants. The trial for the most part became a whitewash, a Pilate-like cleansing of hands. The army closed ranks, and officers who had been vehement in their approba-

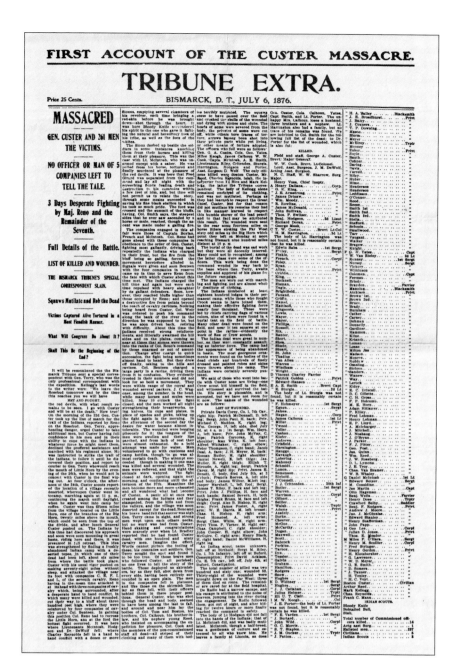

The newspaper reproduced here reads:

FIRST ACCOUNT OF THE CUSTER MASSACRE.

TRIBUNE EXTRA.

Price 25 Cents.　　BISMARCK, D. T., JULY 6, 1876.

MASSACRED

GEN. CUSTER AND 261 MEN THE VICTIMS.

NO OFFICER OR MAN OF 5 COMPANIES LEFT TO TELL THE TALE.

3 Days Desperate Fighting by Maj. Reno and the Remainder of the Seventh.

Full Details of the Battle.

LIST OF KILLED AND WOUNDED.

THE BISMARCK TRIBUNE'S SPECIAL CORRESPONDENT SLAIN.

Squaws Mutilate and Rob the Dead

Victims Captured Alive Tortured in a Most Fiendish Manner.

What Will Congress Do About It?

Shall This Be the Beginning of the End?

"Massacred"

The first account of the battle appeared in an extra edition of the Bismarck Tribune on July 6, 1876. Bismarck lay across and five miles down the Missouri River from Fort Abraham Lincoln, and the men in this casualty list were known personally by the Tribune's readers.

tion of Reno during and immediately after the battle were now reluctant to offer direct criticism; seeking to avoid disgrace for themselves, the regiment, and the army, they modified their stories. Those who told the truth didn't tell the whole truth. The Indians became more numerous, the distances the soldiers traveled longer and more arduous, Custer's orders more vague, and Reno's battle-field decisions more justified. Weir, who might have been bold enough to tell the truth, had died of alcohol-related illnesses a few months after the battle; the only officer critical of Reno was Godfrey, and he worded his testimony carefully, using the words "nervous timidity" rather than "cowardice" to describe Reno's disposition during the battle.

Reno Court of Inquiry

In the hope of clearing his name, Major Marcus Reno requested that an official army court of inquiry be convened. The court met in Chicago on January 13, 1879. Reno is pictured in this newspaper illustration sitting in front of the window on the right.

Lieutenant Edward Settle Godfrey

Godfrey was the only officer from the Seventh Cavalry to even remotely try to criticize Reno's actions at the Little Bighorn. He tempered his claims by stating that Reno displayed "an air of nervous timidity."

Although his officers did not criticize Reno, neither did they commend him. The court's finding was a weak vindication: "The conduct of the officers throughout was excellent, and while subordinates, in some instances, did more for the safety of the command by brilliant displays of courage than did Major Reno, there was nothing in his conduct which requires animadversion from this Court." In the end, the testimony provided by the Reno Court of Inquiry supplied few answers and even more questions about what happened on the Little Bighorn.

The arguments over Custer and his command decisions rage to this day. Some Custerphiles succumb wholly to the Custer myth, that treasure trove of misinformation, tall tales, jingoism, and wishful thinking. To them their patron saint can do no wrong; any negative utterance is chalked up to jealousy and resentment of a brilliant military leader who was in the end betrayed by Reno and Benteen, his two ranking officers—one's ineptness and cowardice, the other's hatred and indifference. Custer becomes for them a martyr, the last cavalier, an icon representing the core American values of self-determination, boldness, vision, and even white supremacy. The Custerphobes, of course, see another man; egotistical, reckless, arrogant, selfish, and tyrannical, he is an insanely ambitious glory-seeker, and later, starting in the 1960s, the brutish Indian butcher who symbolized the injustices white America perpetrated on the noble Native American.

There is truth in both views—though, of course, the real story lies somewhere in between. Much of the factual ammunition used by both sides is based on falsehoods and misinterpretations that have largely derived from sloppy early accounts that twisted some facts and invented others to serve their respective agendas. The debate has been fueled in no small way by the lack of verification and conflicting testimony about what really happened, and why.

Famous Indian Fighters.

Engraved from Photographs expressly for this Work

A.D.WORTHINGTON & CO. HARTFORD CONN.

"Famous Indian Fighters"
Following the nation's horror and outrage over the Battle of the Little Bighorn, Custer was soon placed in the pantheon of great Indian fighters, along with the three men who brought the Great Sioux War to a close: Generals George Crook, Nelson Miles, and Ranald Mackenzie.

So, who was at fault? There is no simple answer.

When Custer's scouts, on several occasions before the battle, warned him that the village was far larger and the warriors more numerous than any previous estimates, Custer waved them off. He had with him more than 700 men, and in his experience, vastly superior forces of Indians panicked and scattered when attacked by a trained, disciplined army unit. His knowledge had been borne out by

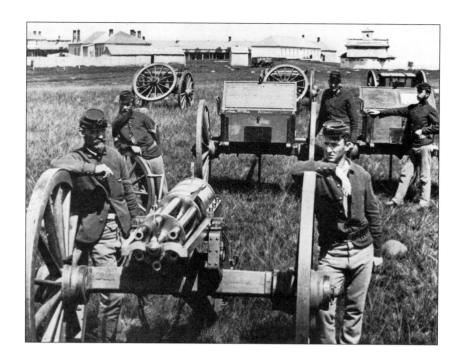

Gatling Guns
Much was made in some quarters of Custer's refusal to take along three Gatling guns offered to him before the Little Bighorn. But the heavy, unwieldy guns were drawn by condemned cavalry mounts and would have slowed down the column considerably over the broken terrain they encountered.

"The New Alliance"
Political cartoonist Charles Nast used Custer's defeat at the Little Bighorn to criticize the government's reduction of the army in this image from July 23, 1876.

virtually every Indian encounter of any size in recent memory. The Indians simply did not stand and fight, and furthermore rarely fought as a cohesive, organized unit. Even if there were 2,000 or more warriors, the Seventh Cavalry could handle them. Custer said more than once that there weren't enough Indians on the continent to defeat his Seventh Cavalry.

Custer underestimated the size of his enemy, but not by much—he personally thought there might be as many as 1,500, not far off the 1,800 to 2,000 he may have fought. He made a more costly underestimation of the Indians's determination, confidence, and fury. They were also well-led and well-armed. Although a supply of ammunition was often a problem for them, quite a few Indians owned rifles of all kinds, and as many as 200 may have carried the Henry and Winchester repeaters; because it was thought that most Indian fighting would be done at long distance on the vast plains, the cavalry standard-issue rifle was the 1873 single-shot Springfield. And Custer knew nothing of Crook's defeat on the Rosebud a week earlier in which a smaller number of warriors than were at Little Bighorn fought a larger army unit to a standstill.

Lack of effective reconnaissance was another mistake. Custer's decision to attack on June 25, prompted by his belief that the Seventh's presence had been discovered, curtailed any long-range scouting—reconnaissance that would have almost certainly contributed valuable intelligence. As it was, the Seventh rode into battle knowing little of the enemy's exact location or size. If Custer's scouts had had another day to reconnoiter, Benteen's trek to the west would have been unnecessary, and a more effective battle plan could have been formulated, rather than the one Custer concocted on the fly.

And more thorough reconnaissance would surely have warned Custer of another underestimated foe—the terrain. The jagged bluffs and ridges Custer ultimately traversed and on which he made his final stand was no place for a cavalry battle, but it was excellent cover for the greatest guerrilla fighters of all time, the Plains Indians. Had Custer avoided that terrain, he and his cavalry may not have been annihilated.

Perhaps no written military orders ever put to paper have been the subject of more discussion than those General Terry delivered to Custer on the morning of June 22. Aware that Custer was still smarting from his humiliation by President Grant, Terry couched his orders in tactful terms that suggested rather than demanded. Although delicately worded, they were not entirely discretionary—though that is how Custer apparently understood them, and not without good reason. In one sentence, the general specifically directed him to continue up the Rosebud as far as the headwaters of the Tongue before turning toward the Little Bighorn—even if Custer struck the Indian trail. But surrounding that fairly straightforward sentence were plenty of indefinite suggestions and allowances for Custer's own choices, enough leeway that there is little doubt Custer gave the orders short shrift: "It is, of course, impossible to give you any definite instructions in regard to this movement, and were it not impossible to do so the Department Commander places too much confidence in your zeal, energy, and ability to wish to impose upon you precise orders which might hamper your action when nearly in contact with the enemy." He went on to say: "He desires that you should conform to them unless you shall see sufficient reason for departing from them." That was all Custer needed. There was no mention of a combined attack by his and Gibbon's column on June 26. "It was announced by General Terry that General Custer's column would strike the blow," wrote Major Brisbin in an article in the *New York Herald* on July 8, 1876.

That appeared to be everyone else's view as well. After the summit meeting on board the *Far West*, Lieutenant James H. Bradley, Gibbon's capable chief of scouts, wrote in his diary on June 21: "It is understood that if Custer arrives first he is at liberty to attack at once if he deems prudent. We have little hope of being in at the death, as Custer will undoubtedly exert himself to the utmost to get there first and win all the laurels for himself and his regiment." Even Terry, writing to Sheridan on June 21, admitted, "I only hope that one of the two columns will find the Indians. I go personally with Gibbon." The general would not have offered Custer the use of four more troops of cavalry and the Gatlings unless he felt sure that Custer would be the one to hit the hostiles first.

Though Custer has been criticized for disobeying the letter of Terry's orders, he would have been roundly condemned if he had let the Indians slip away when they were only a day's march away.

Major Marcus A. Reno
Although he was officially exonerated of blame in the fate of Custer and his men at the Little Bighorn, Reno's end was sad and lonely.

Captain Frederick W. Benteen
To the end of his days, Benteen never stopped hating and criticizing Custer.

Right: **Red Horse**
The Indians won the Battle of the Little Bighorn, but they would ultimately lose the war. Red Horse's small band of Minneconjou was defeated in a surprise attack by General George Crook at Slim Buttes in Dakota Territory on September 9, 1876.

Above: **Little Wolf and Dull Knife**
The village of Cheyenne chiefs Little Wolf (left) and Dull Knife on the Red Fork of the Powder River was destroyed by Colonel Ranald S. Mackenzie on November 25, 1876. With their village went most of their possessions and winter food and clothing, ultimately forcing them to surrender on April 24, 1877, at the Red Cloud Agency.

Another full day spent heading south would chance the Indians' getting wind of the Seventh or Gibbon's column or both; the hostiles might even have broke camp, headed north, and overwhelmed the much smaller column of Gibbon's. Even if that hadn't happened, the entire campaign would have been wasted. Custer saw his mission as to find the hostiles and attack them, so he followed the Indian sign across the Rosebud divide. It was the pivotal decision of the campaign.

Custer has been criticized for his refusal of the battery of three Gatlings, but there was nothing wrong with that. The Gatlings would never have kept up with the cavalry, or even the pack train that followed. As a matter of fact, they straggled behind Terry's infantry over the next few days. But Custer's refusal to accept Terry's offer of

Little Big Man

A longtime lieutenant of Crazy Horse, Little Big Man surrendered at Fort Robinson, Nebraska, with the Oglala war leader in May 1877. Little Big Man later played a role in the death of his leader when Crazy Horse was bayoneted by a soldier.

were within communicating distance of one another. The lack of a coordinated time and place for the attack at the Little Bighorn, which was to come from (at various times) two or three or four widely separated battalions, made it tragically clear how Custer misjudged the Indians' fighting abilities and temperament. And that may have been his biggest mistake of all.

Custer's primary mistakes—his overconfidence in the Seventh's abilities, and a low opinion of those of the Lakota—were compounded by a more subtle one. He most likely possessed a plan and vision of how he and the Seventh would defeat the Indians and go on to everlasting glory. Unfortunately, not everyone subscribed to his personal vision, and chief among the disbelievers were the two most important members of his command—Reno and Benteen. These two senior officers failed him, Reno most glaringly. Not because he stopped his charge several hundred yards short of the camp—his small force and its tired mounts would probably have been swallowed up by the extensive village, which was quickly arming itself as Reno and his battalion thundered down the valley. His decision to halt and form a skirmish line made sense. So did his move into the stand of timber along the river a short time later. His outnumbered Indian scouts on the left flank fought for a short time, captured some ponies, and then left, leaving the left flank to be overwhelmed by increasing numbers of hostiles. But his leadership on the skirmish line was almost nonexistent, and his panicked troopers exercised little fire control, expending a large portion of their ammunition quickly and without results. His performance in the wood wasn't any better. It was his panicked decision to flee the relatively strong position of the trees without his wounded and almost twenty other men, and his poor handling of that disorganized, uncovered retreat, that doomed Custer. The complete rout of Reno's battalion released many hundreds of warriors to turn and hurry north to fling themselves against the bluecoats downstream. The Indians would otherwise have had to divide their forces, and they would have also had to help the women and children break down the village and scatter, since that order had already been given. Finally, Reno's frightened appearance and blind panic had spread to the men in his command. By the time they reached the bluffs across the river, they were dazed, demoralized, and scared, and incapable of rendering any immediate assistance to Custer's force.

Benteen, too, failed Custer and his five companies. He was disgruntled over orders that he would later brand as "senseless . . . valley hunting ad infinitum"—orders which, at least in his mind, relegated him to a minor role. He believed that Custer had sent him on a wild goose chase to keep him out of the real fight. But his company subaltern, Lieutenant Francis M. Gibson, wrote after the battle that the orders were clear: "Benteen's battalion was sent to the left about 5 miles to see if the Indians were trying to escape up the

Custer's primary mistakes were compounded by a more subtle one. He most likely possessed a plan and vision of how he and the Seventh would defeat the Indians and go on to everlasting glory. Unfortunately, not everyone subscribed to his personal vision, and chief among the disbelievers were the two most important members of his command—Major Marcus Reno and Captain Frederick Benteen.

valley of the Little Big Horn, after which we were to hurry and rejoin the command as soon as possible," and Benteen himself, in his official report, corroborated that. After confirming that Indians were not visible in the valley, he turned his battalion around and headed back to the main trail. Just as they reached the main Indian trail, they were passed by Boston Custer, riding from the pack train toward the Little Big Horn to reach his brother's command. He would reach his brothers just after trumpeter Martin was sent back, in plenty of time to fight and die with them. Clearly Benteen's battalion was not far behind the rest of the Seventh, probably only half an hour when he hit the main trail. But the time lag increased from there due to his slow pace. Two urgent messages from Custer ordering him to hurry couldn't persuade him to move his battalion much past a trot. Benteen kept a leisurely pace back, and spent a long time watering the horses at a morass—so long that Captain Weir and other officers expressed their impatience after the sound of distant firing was heard. From there the pace was a slow trot until Sergeant Kanipe galloped up with his spoken orders for Benteen to "come quick—a big Indian camp." Benteen picked it up a bit for the next mile, until Martin rode up and delivered his written orders urging Benteen to "Be quick." His response was to take a somewhat faster pace, but he did not order a gallop until the firing ahead of them became more pronounced and they were almost upon Reno Hill. And when he joined up with Reno's terrorized command soon after, he elected to remain with Reno rather than follow his direct orders to join Custer. The time then was approximately 4:20 P.M.—about the same time that the major part of the battle four miles away was just beginning, and more than an hour before the carnage would be finished.

Even with his dawdling on the back trail, Benteen still could

Sitting Bull and Buffalo Bill Cody

When Sitting Bull and less than 200 ragged and starving followers rode into Fort Buford in Dakota Territory to surrender on July 19, 1881, it marked the end of the Great Sioux War. Sitting Bull later joined Buffalo Bill Cody's Wild West show for the 1885 season. Cody paid him fifty dollars a week and treated him with respect.

likely have made a dramatic difference in the Custer fight if he had left Reno Hill then and there and raced to Custer's aid. He did not. Admittedly, Reno seemed to be in desperate need of help, the vulnerable pack train was somewhere to the rear, and Custer, everyone thought, could take care of himself. Custer's aura of invulnerability was such that even Benteen, who hated him, fell victim to it.

In the end, the reasons for the debacle were larger than a few individuals. As one prominent Custer historian put it, the Indians' "numbers had been underestimated; their leadership and fighting capacity undervalued; their superiority in arms not even suspected. The 7th Cavalry paid the penalty for national stupidity."

One more overriding factor must be mentioned: Custer's Luck. It finally ran out.

The Plains Indians' greatest military triumph would, ironically, spell the end of their freedom as well.

After the news of Custer's defeat at the Little Bighorn spread, volunteer groups sprung up across the country, eager for revenge on the "bloodthirsty savages" responsible. The Little Bighorn defeat had been more than a disaster. The fact that a large, well-equipped force had lost to "undisciplined savages" — cowards, in the eyes of a public who had nothing but contempt for the Indians' standard combat strategies of hit-and-run and ambush — was a humiliation not only to the U.S. Army, but to the entire country. The fact that the news arrived at the moment that the country was celebrating its centennial made it a national embarrassment, and the country demanded revenge. Reservations in the northern plains were placed under military control. On August 15, 1876, Congress passed a law compelling the Lakota to part with the Black Hills and the Powder River and Bighorn country, and they were forced to move onto reservations before receiving further provisions. Red Cloud, Spotted Tail, and other chiefs signed the agreement, for they had no choice — their people were starving. The army then took the agency Indians' horses and arms. Now all the Lakota's country belonged to the white man.

After leaving their Little Bighorn camp, the triumphant Indians headed leisurely south toward the Bighorn Mountains. The number of Indian casualties was never accurately determined, though estimates from 32 to almost 300 were made; the terrified bluecoats had exercised little fire control and had been bad shots. After traveling about fifteen miles the massive camp split up, small groups leaving to return to the reservations or to hunt on their own. Through July and August, the villages moved east to the Rosebud and the Tongue, then the Powder and the Little Missouri Rivers, with more groups breaking off along the way. Sitting Bull's Hunkpapas headed north down the Little Missouri, and Crazy Horse's Oglalas and the Cheyennes up the river south.

The army had gained new respect for the Indians, and they waited almost two months for reinforcements before venturing after the hostiles. Crook's column was reinforced with ten companies of cavalry under Colonel Wesley Merritt and started north along Rosebud Creek, 2,000 men strong. Custer's old scout-turned-showman, Buffalo Bill Cody, closed his show at the Philadelphia Centennial Exposition, saying his services were needed in the West, and joined Crook. Terry and Gibbon's column marched south down the Yellowstone with 1,600 men. The plan was to crush the hostiles between them. The two reinforced columns met on the Rosebud on August 10 without sighting the Lakota. Crook's small victory at Slim Buttes against Red Horse's people on September 9 was the only good news he could claim; Terry and Gibbon never even saw a hostile Indian. Meanwhile, a column of 500 men under Colonel Nelson Miles was chasing Sitting Bull all over Montana with little to show for their efforts.

The severity of the Indian problem was such that a winter campaign was decided upon, and in November, the Powder River Expedition was organized. Colonels Ranald Mackenzie and Merritt were also reassigned to Crook's force with their cavalry commands, and in late October they captured two large camps, one of them Red Cloud's, who had left his agency in August. The force drove toward the Bighorn Mountains, and on November 25, near the Powder River's Red Fork, the efficient Mackenzie mounted a surprise dawn attack on Dull Knife's large Cheyenne village of 200 lodges. Forty Indians died, while the rest escaped. But the loss of most of their horses and possessions, including their winter shelter, food, and clothing, dealt a mortal blow to the Cheyenne, who walked east through below-zero weather toward Crazy Horse on the Powder. Two weeks later, they found him, and the Oglalas shared their already meager stores. But the winter was severe, and the hungry Indians suffered greatly. A New Year's Day attack by Miles resulted in few casualties but wiped out much of the Indians' remaining supplies. Throughout the winter, small bands of Lakota and Cheyenne limped into the Red Cloud and Spotted Tail Agencies. Dull Knife and 524 Cheyennes surrendered on April 24, 1877, at the Red Cloud Agency.

Finally, Crazy Horse decided his people had suffered enough. He led his band of almost 900 people into Fort Robinson, Nebraska, and surrendered. To Lieutenant William H. Clark, who oversaw Red Cloud Agency, he said, "Friend, I shake with this hand because my heart is on this side; I want this peace to last forever." But both Indian peace factions and the army were fearful of his power and considered him too dangerous to remain free. Crook ordered him imprisoned, and on September 6, 1877, he was brought under guard to the army compound at the fort. When he saw that the soldiers were trying to imprison him, he struggled to break free. Little Big

"Friend, I shake with this hand because my heart is on this side; I want this peace to last forever."
—Crazy Horse, upon surrendering to Lieutenant William H. Clark at Red Cloud Agency

The Ghost Dance

In 1889, news came to the Plains Indians from the Nevada Territory of a young Paiute named Wovoka who had fallen into a trance and awoken with a miraculous message. He had seen the spirit world, he said, and received a revelation. Wonderful things were in store for the Indian people in the coming years. The buffalo would return, the Indians' dead ancestors would arise, and those alive would live forever. And the white man would disappear.

To evoke this promised land, followers had to follow a strict doctrine of peace that preached against war, fighting, stealing, lying, and cruelty, and they had to perform a dance that Wovoka said had been taught to him in the next world. This "Ghost Dance," as it was called by whites, was simple: Dancers shuffled in a circle while singing songs about the coming redemption. The object was to enter a trance considered a deathlike state, therein to view briefly the wonderful all-Indian world to come.

The demoralized and downtrodden Indians found Wovoka's apocalyptic vision irresistible, and flocked to it in droves. A Lakota warrior and mystic named Kicking Bear brought the Ghost Dance to the poverty-stricken Sioux agencies—and introduced an element of violence to the new religion, indicating that the disappearance of the *wasichus* might be hastened. The Lakota added another wrinkle: Dancers wore loose shirts that were considered bulletproof.

The "ghost shirts" alarmed whites, who reasoned that the bulletproof garments indicated a mass uprising; some speeches by leaders of the movement reinforced their conclusions. Settlers in towns near the reservations insisted on protection, and near the end of November 1890, army units were posted to the Pine Ridge Reservation in South Dakota. The army's presence enraged the Indians there, and tensions escalated alarmingly. After Sitting Bull—who was perceived by the army to be a leader of the cult and a barrier to any peace plans—was killed by Indian policemen in a botched attempt to arrest him on December 14, things went from bad to worse. Groups of Lakota fled to the camp of the

Ghost Dancers

Minneconjou Big Foot, another leader deemed a troublemaker by the government and marked for arrest. After several days of evading the army, his band of 350—mostly women and children—surrendered on December 28 to a squadron of the Seventh Cavalry. They camped twenty miles south of Pine Ridge next to a creek named Wounded Knee.

During the night, the army squad was reinforced to almost 500 men. In the morning, the troopers surrounded and began to disarm the captives. It was decided that force was necessary, and the result was catastrophic. While a medicine man performed the Ghost Dance and exhorted his people to resist, tensions on both sides mounted. The situation erupted when one Indian shot a rifle off, and the nervous soldiers responded with a point-blank volley that killed half the warriors. The rest pulled out concealed weapons and attacked the bluecoats. An all-out massacre ensued. Four rapid-fire Hotchkiss guns raked masses of Indians, including fleeing women and children. In less than an hour of murderous close-range carnage, about half the Indians were killed and fifty more wounded. The army had twenty-five killed and thirty-nine wounded.

After one more battle in 1890 at Drexel Mission, South Dakota, the rest of the rebellious Indians surrendered on January 15, 1891. The Ghost Dance soon disappeared as quickly as it had arrived.

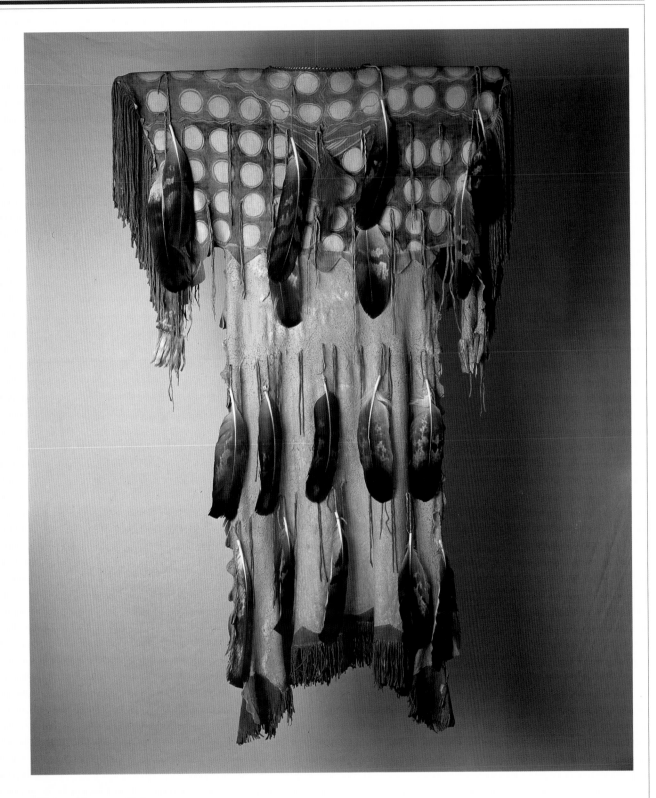

Ghost Dance Shirt

Made circa 1885 by Arapaho Indians at the height of the Ghost Dance movement, this shirt was believed to protect its wearer from the bullets of the white men. The shirt was later purchased from a Ghost Dance follower by a European settler in 1916.

Man, once one of Crazy Horse's most loyal warriors but now a policeman for the army, pinned his arms behind him. In the scuffle that followed, Crazy Horse was bayoneted twice by a soldier named William Gentle, and died that night. "It is well," said another chief, "he has looked for death and it has come."

The last of the hostile Lakota were defeated when Miles overwhelmed a small band of Minneconjous led by Lame Deer near the Tongue River on May 7. That left only Sitting Bull, who had led his Hunkpapas north to Canada, arriving there on May 5. Two thousand Oglalas had left Red Cloud Agency after Crazy Horse's death to join Sitting Bull, but the herds of buffalo dwindled, the winters were fierce, and Canadian tribes such as the Blackfeet threatened them. Small parties crossed back across the border steadily over the next few years. Finally, on July 19, 1881, Sitting Bull and less than 200 followers, starving and in rags, rode into Fort Buford in Dakota Territory and surrendered. The Great Sioux War had come to a close.

Sitting Bull was imprisoned for two years, then allowed to join his Hunkpapas at the Standing Rock Agency in Dakota Territory. A few years later, Buffalo Bill Cody invited him to join his Wild West show. Sitting Bull toured as its star attraction for one season and became friends with Cody. He later returned to Standing Rock and became a leader in the Ghost Dance, a spiritual movement that was misunderstood and feared by whites. The army ordered him to be taken into custody, and early on December 15, 1890, he was shot simultaneously in the chest and the back of the head by an Indian policeman while resisting arrest. He died immediately.

Two weeks later, the massacre of Sitting Bull's band at Wounded Knee by remnants of the Seventh Cavalry wrote an ugly ending to the Sioux War of 1876.

Though the Court of Inquiry officially exonerated him, Reno was ostracized by his fellow officers, who had only defended him to protect the good name of the regiment. Less than a year after the Little Bighorn he was brought up on charges of forcing his attentions on another officer's wife, and then attempting to punish her for refusing him. He was judged guilty and sentenced to be dismissed from the army, but the sentence was reduced to a two-year suspension from rank and pay. After reinstatement, Reno's drinking soon got him in trouble on several occasions. He was finally dishonorably discharged due to "conduct unbecoming an officer and an gentleman"—he was caught redhanded as a peeping tom looking into his CO's house at the CO's daughter, with whom Reno was smitten. He drifted into obscurity after that, and died of cancer in 1890, penniless, bitter, and forgotten. In the twentieth century, some historians of the battle would argue for a more sympathetic look at his actions. Almost eighty years later, in 1967, his dishonorable discharge was reversed,

Libbie Custer
Photographed here in 1900, Libbie Custer remained a tireless crusader honoring the memory of her husband. She died April 6, 1933, two days before her ninety-first birthday.

The massacre of Sitting Bull's band at Wounded Knee by remnants of the Seventh Cavalry wrote an ugly ending to the Sioux War of 1876.

citing as reason for his erratic behavior "the recent loss of his wife, his state of bachelorhood in a desolate frontier fort and in the field and the attendant primitive conditions."

Benteen, the hero of Reno Hill, was promoted to major several years later and transferred to the Ninth Cavalry, but his drinking, once controlled, became constant and excessive. He was court-martialed; after overwhelming testimony regarding his frequent drunkenness, he was found guilty. The court took pity on him and allowed him to take an honorable discharge for medical reasons. He lived comfortably another ten years in Atlanta. The irascible soldier got crustier as he aged, and he never stopped hating Custer—and thinking of him almost constantly. As Custer's star rose in the public mind, and his faded, he took every opportunity to discredit his former commander.

Elizabeth Bacon Custer outlived her beloved Autie by almost fifty-seven years. She never remarried. The remainder of her life was primarily spent gilding the memory and reputation of her husband. She wrote three books chronicling their lives together in the army, and all sold well. While she was never rich, she became affluent enough to travel around the world, winter in Florida, buy a cottage in the Catskills, a house in New York City, and several other places. She moved frequently. She never stopped writing, petitioning, and influencing in her husband's name. She died on April 6, 1933, two days before her ninety-first birthday, and was buried next to her Armstrong at West Point, on a green hill above the Hudson River.

George Armstrong Custer, of course, achieved immortality.

Reconciliation
At a ceremony in 1926 on the fiftieth anniversary of the Battle of the Little Bighorn, White Bull and General Edward Settle Godfrey bury the hatchet.

CUSTER'S LAST STAND

Chapter 10

Legend

*"Desperate and glorious—aye, in defeat
most desperate, most glorious,
After thy many battles, in which, never
yielding up a gun or a color,
Leaving behind thee a memory
sweet to soldiers,
Thou yieldest up thyself."*
—Walt Whitman, "A Death-Sonnet for Custer"

Immortality is one thing, greatness another. Custer achieved the first, but under the harsh, cold light of objectivity, fell short of the later. Despite a brilliant Civil War record, his career as an Indian fighter was erratic; only toward the end of his career—before the Little Bighorn, ironically—did he begin to understand the special demands of Indian warfare and comprehend Indian combat strategy. But the way he lived, the way he looked, and, most importantly, the way he died—combined with a few other serendipitous factors and a final twist of Custer's Luck—made him immortal. And he ascended to

Custer's Last Stand Re-Enactment
The most popular part of Buffalo Bill Cody's Wild West show was the dramatic re-enactment of Custer's Last Stand. This poster dates from 1904.

the pantheon of American myths as quickly as he had risen to the rank of general in the Civil War—which is to say, like a comet.

While the young nation in the midst of its centennial celebration reeled at the news of Custer's defeat and raged at the thought that the loss had been at the hands of undisciplined savages, the ironies of the theme of the Exposition in Philadelphia, "a Century of Progress," seemed painfully clear. At the same time, Custer's Last Stand became a rallying point for Americans in need of inspiration, for the truth was that, for all the wondrous scientific wizardry displayed at the Exposition, 1876 had not been a year of American triumph. Between the Belknap scandal, the severe aftershocks of the Panic of 1873, and the exposure of the Whiskey Ring and other evidence of government corruption, the national character seemed tarnished, its moral fiber weakened. The stark heroism of Custer and his command seized the imagination of the American public. "The charge of Custer is an answer to it all," opined the *New York Herald* of the country's moral stumbling. "It shows that manhood and valor, self-denial and absolute consecration of duty, even at the sacrifice of life, all remain with us."

On July 10, 1876, only a few days after the story of Custer's death hit the Eastern papers, poet Walt Whitman's "A Death-Sonnet for Custer" was published in the *New York Tribune*:

> . . . Thou of the sunny, flowing hair, in battle,
> I erewhile now, with erect head, pressing ever in
>   front, bearing a bright sword in thy hand,
> Now ending well the splendid fever of thy deeds,
> (I bring no dirge for it or thee—I bring a glad,
>   triumphal sonnet;)
>   There in the far northwest, in struggle, charge, and
>   saber-smite,
> Desperate and glorious—aye, in defeat most desperate,
>   most glorious,
> After thy many battles, in which, never yielding up a
>   gun or a color,
> Leaving behind thee a memory sweet to soldiers,
> Thou yieldest up thyself.

It would not rank with Whitman's best, but it was better than many of the poetic encomiums that would follow from Henry Wadsworth Longfellow, John Greenleaf Whittier, William Cullen Bryant, and countless others—none of which are remembered today. While politicians and generals argued over blame, a public desperate for a sign of destiny was primed to deify Custer.

A dime novelist who began scribbling away at his own tribute soon after the Boy General's death virtually etched in stone the Custer myth as it was known for decades thereafter. Frederick

Poet Walt Whitman
Whitman's poem eulogizing Custer was perhaps not his greatest work, but did help ensure Custer's popularity and immortality.

Whittaker had enlisted as a private and rose to the rank of lieutenant in the Army of the Potomac's Cavalry Corps. Though he never met Custer personally during the Civil War, he was able to observe him in action many times as, for a short while, they served in the same division. In 1871, Whittaker began writing dime and nickel novels, eventually churning out eighty-two of them in a fifteen-year span. He finally met Custer in the offices of *Galaxy*, the magazine that published several of the general's articles. After Custer's death, Whittaker wrote an impassioned article for *Galaxy* praising Custer and defending his actions on the Little Bighorn. The New York publishers of Custer's *My Life on the Plains* were impressed, and asked him to write a biography. Whittaker turned to Libbie Custer to help. She seized upon this chance to vindicate her husband's name and worked closely with the author, even sharing much of the General's private correspondence with him.

Whittaker worked fast, and his *A Complete Life of Gen. George A. Custer* appeared a week and a half before Christmas 1876. "His life was a perfect romance," gushed an ad for the book. The lengthy—two inches thick!—illustrated tome was a complete whitewash; it lifted great chunks of its text from *My Life on the Plains*, and sported a healthy share of misconceptions, factual errors, and just plain fabrications that would come to be accepted as truth. But it was well-written, if a bit florid, and the battle scenes especially were handled with flair. Whittaker also raised a small storm of controversy that would endure to this day when—persuaded by Libbie, no doubt—he claimed that the tragic end met by Custer and his command was the result of Reno's cowardice and Benteen's refusal to ride quickly to Custer's aid as ordered. Though the blame had previously been placed in large part on the Boy General's shoulders, public opinion swung around in the glamorous Custer's favor once the initial shock wore off.

The book sold well, and was instrumental in codifying and perpetuating the Custer myth. Virtually every treatment of the battle since its publication owes it a debt of gratitude, for within its pages were all the significant elements: Custer's humble, small-town beginnings; his Horatio Alger-esque pluck in securing an appointment to West Point; his extraordinary bravery and bold leadership on the battlefield; his subsequent glories against the Indians in the West; and his noble command's Last Stand, outnumbered and resolute, on a hill against overwhelming odds, their charismatic leader surrounded by a circle of his loyal men, cut down in the prime of life. Whittaker's vision of Custer as a knight in shining armor would boost him to the level of legend and hold sway for more than fifty years—until, not coincidentally, the death of Libbie Custer.

A Complete Life of Gen. George A. Custer became, both in terms of its story elements and its complete affirmation of Custer's nobility, the basic source for many other books, poems, stories, plays, and

Overleaf: *Custer's Last Fight*
This epic painting of the Battle of the Little Bighorn played an enormous role in establishing the Custer myth. Created by artist Cassilly Adams in 1886, the original oil painting measured an astonishing 9½ by 16½ feet. It eventually was mounted on the wall of a St. Louis, Missouri, barroom, and was acquired by the Anheuser-Busch, Inc., brewery in a claims settlement. Anheuser-Busch directed artist F. Otto Becker to repaint and lithograph the image in 1895; in the process, Becker made many revisions to Adams's original. In 1896, the brewery firm began reproducing the lithograph as promotion for its Budweiser beer, and more than a quarter million copies are estimated to have been reproduced since. The lithograph has hung in saloons and barrooms across the country, inspiring an indelible image of Custer's Last Stand.

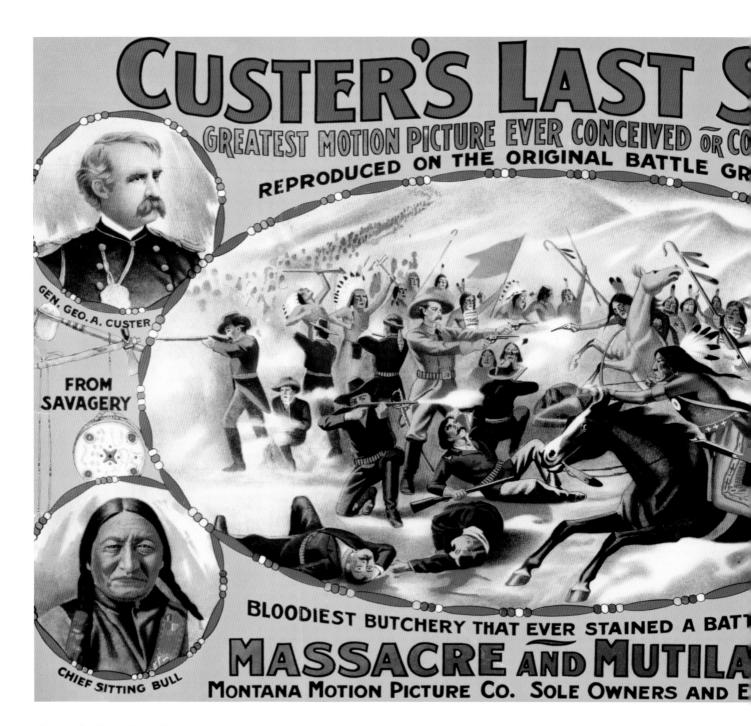

Custer's Last Stand

Montana Motion Picture Company's Custer's Last Stand *(probably a reissue of* On the Little Big Horn, 1909*) boasted that it was shot on the actual Little Bighorn battlefield. This poster gleefully noted that it was the "Bloodiest Butchery That Ever Stained A Battlefield" and titillated viewers with "Massacre and Mutilation."*

Custer's Last Fight

"The Greatest Wild West Feature Ever Filmed" proclaimed this advertising one-sheet for Thomas H. Ince's ambitious 1912 portrayal of the Custer myth. Publicity for the movie promised "Thrilling Charges . . . Sensational Hand-to-Hand Conflicts . . . The Indian 'Circle of Death' . . . The Last Stand of Custer on the Hill . . . The Most Thrilling Film Ever Seen, Costing More Than $30,000.00."

*On the Little Big Horn; or,
Custer's Last Stand*
*Custer leapt onto the silver screen
early, and several silent films were
made of the Last Stand. William
Selig's* On the Little Big Horn *was,
in 1909, the first. It portrayed
Custer as America's hero, the
epitome of courage and nobility. As
this pre-release poster promised, "A
Picture Full of the Pathos that
Grips the Heart."*

Tenting on the Plains (1893) did as much as
Whittaker's to spread the gospel of her heroic
cavalier. But legends and myths, and the ways
they are viewed and used, change with the times,
and Custer was no different. After Libbie's death,
the public's perception of Custer, largely one of
unquestioned admiration, underwent a transfor-
mation. The hard times of the Depression bred a
new cynicism in the land, and debunking was the
order of the day. Custer's historical reassessment
was startling.

Novelist Frederic F. Van de Water's icono-
clastic biography *Glory-Hunter* burst on the scene
in 1935. A vivid portrait of Custer as an immature
egotist sacrificing his men and himself in a
reckless pursuit of glory, it ushered in a host of
revisionist examinations of the Boy General, such
as Fred Dustin's *The Custer Tragedy* (1939). A
newly sympathetic attitude toward the American
Indian accentuated and accelerated this change.
The novels *Bugles in the Afternoon* (1944) by
Ernest Haycox, Will Henry's *No Survivors* (1950),
and Thomas Berger's *Little Big Man* (1964)
represented the fictional highpoints of this brand
of debunking. As the twentieth century wore on,
biographers repeatedly attempted to come to grips
with this dual personality, a schism that reflected,
in many ways, America's own. By the end of the century, Custer had
inspired more words than any other American except Abraham
Lincoln.

The silver screen, more a means of pure escapism than the
printed word, took longer to reveal Custer's dark side. Since the first
incarnation of the battle onscreen, in a 1909 William Selig production entitled *On the Little Big Horn; or, Custer's Last Stand*, the
subject has been a popular one—and almost entirely positive regarding Custer's character. Selig's film included footage he shot of a
reenactment of the Last Stand on the actual battlefield, with the
scout Curley reproducing his role of the Lone Survivor of the battle.
Three years later, *Custer's Last Fight*, Thomas H. Ince's even more
ambitious epic, appeared. The three-reel film featured 2,000 soldiers
and Indians, and was billed as "the most colossal and sensational War
Picture in the Entire History of Motion Pictures," which really
wasn't much of a claim in the early days of cinema. *The Flaming
Frontier* of 1926, fifty years after the original battle, was a first-class
affair starring matinee idols Hoot Gibson and Dustin Farnum and "a
cast of thousands." Though it was hardly a classic, high production
values, nonstop action, and a smart publicity campaign helped make
it one of the year's biggest successes.

But the definitive screen Custer would not appear until 1941, in *They Died With Their Boots On*. Chief among its assets was the brilliant casting of Errol Flynn as the Boy General. There could have been no better choice: The handsome Flynn had portrayed swashbuckling characters in hugely successful films such as *Captain Blood, The Charge of the Light Brigade, The Sea Hawk*, and *The Adventures of Robin Hood*, and he had established his western credentials in *Dodge City, Virginia City*, and *Santa Fe Trail*. Flynn's portrayal of Custer as a charismatic rebel was tremendously appealing to a nation on the brink of world war, and the climactic (though highly unlikely) scene of the buckskin-clad general standing alone on a hill with only a saber in his hand, ready to defiantly meet his fate, remains one of the most memorable images in all of film.

The debunking of the Boy General finally reached the screen in 1948, in an indirect way. Postwar cynicism allowed and encouraged darker looks at heroes and patriotism, and the western saw its share. Director John Ford changed the names and places in that year's *Fort Apache*—Custer becomes Lieutenant Colonel Owen Thursday, and the Lakota were now Apaches—and for the first time Custer's portrayal reflects the cold, egotistical martinet depicted in Van de Water's *Glory-Hunter*. (Ford, ever the sentimentalist, allows his "hero," played by Henry Fonda, a measure of personal redemption in the end.)

The 1950s and 1960s saw several mediocre movies about the battle, including *Little Big Horn, Warpath, Bugles in the Afternoon, Sitting Bull, 7th Cavalry, Tonka, The Glory Guys, The Great Sioux Massacre*, and the ambitious though flawed *Custer of the West;* Robert Shaw's Custer in that film is the most complex, balanced, and probably most accurate portrayal of the general yet seen onscreen. A few of these films offered a less-than-heroic Custer, but it wasn't until Arthur Penn's *Little Big Man* (1970), based on the Thomas Berger novel, that Hollywood came close to capturing Van de Water's madman onscreen. The film's protagonist is 121-year-old Jack Crabb, who remembers his life as a pioneer, adopted Indian, and sole survivor of Custer's Last Stand, and for the most part the film is immensely entertaining. Times had certainly changed, however: For the first time, America's brutal treatment of the Indian is shown as genocidal, and Custer is portrayed as a borderline psycho who embarks on a long, rambling monologue as his end approaches. Richard Mulligan's Custer is a memorable creation and a relevant symbol of the zeitgeist of the 1970s, but he's also over the top and one-note—he's so much a message of the times that he's now charmingly quaint, like bell-bottoms or hippies, and there's little of the balance seen in *Custer of the West*. Worth mentioning, finally, is the 1991 two-part TV movie *Son of the Morning Star*, based on Evan S. Connell's fair-minded, best-selling book. Although Rosanna Arquette was miscast as Libbie, Gary Cole made a well-shaded Custer, and the production boasted excellent photography, a fine cast, and an

The debunking of the Boy General finally reached the screen in 1948, in an indirect way. Postwar cynicism allowed and encouraged darker looks at heroes and patriotism, and the western saw its share.

Right: **The Definitive Custer**
The silver screen's definitive Custer, Errol Flynn, in They Died With Their Boots On, *stands amongst the dead on the Little Bighorn battlefield.*

Facing page: ***They Died With Their Boots On***

intelligent script. The latest entry in the Custer film sweepstakes, though not definitive, was well worth watching.

Though the true Custer remains elusive on screen and in print—indeed, in every cultural depiction—that interest has not slowed. An army of passionate Custerphiles and Custerphobes, and those few battle buffs uncommitted to either camp, still debate the most esoteric aspects of the subject; there is probably more activity today in that respect than at any other time. Chief among the reasons for this enduring interest is the mystery. No one will ever know exactly what happened on that hot Sunday afternoon in Montana. Complicating that unassailable fact is a host of others that are more problematic: Time after time, the same incident will be reported by three or four eyewitnesses as happening in a very different way. Like the movie *Rashomon*, every observer's version of an event is differ-ent—but not necessarily untrue. It's hell on history, but heaven to history buffs. Each student of the battle can see what he or she wants to see. The debate, and the interest, will never end.

Little Big Man

Richard Mulligan as a certifiably crazy Custer in Arthur Penn's Little Big Man.

The legend of Custer has itself spawned several other corollary legends. The claim that Rain in the Face cut out Custer's heart . . . that Custer committed suicide . . . or that he was killed early on, down at the river, and never participated in the Last Stand . . . All these and others gained believers based on widely circulated falsehoods, distortions, and half-truths. Like the fictitious saber that Custer brandished in most early visual depictions, these rumors had a life of their own that refused to bow to anything as trivial as the truth.

One of the more persistent stories that cropped up almost immediately after the Battle of the Little Bighorn was that of the lone survivor—a man who rode with Custer but somehow survived to view Custer's final moments and live to tell the tale. Invariably, the storyteller relates an ingenious tale of how he escaped the horrific fate of the doomed cavalrymen. One man claimed he was sent by Custer for medical supplies; another had been assigned to look after the officers' baggage. Some hid under dead horses, others under or inside dead buffalo. One self-proclaimed survivor of the Last Stand said he hit his head when his horse fell, causing him to lose his memory for twenty-four years. Each of these "survivors" affirmed the public's perception that Custer and his men fought valiantly to the end.

Besides the accounts of these claimants—a number that had reached seventy by 1939, according to one writer—the legend popped up frequently in popular fiction. An interesting variation occurred in the juvenile fiction of the late 1800s, in which a youth in the guise of a trumpeter, scout, or messenger, who somehow strikes up a friendship with Custer, misses out on the final battle or escapes at the last second. Adult fiction about the subject more often depended on a disgraced officer of the Seventh Cavalry who clears his name or regains his honor at the Little Bighorn. A curious combination of both fact and fiction were several dime novels featuring pulp-fiction hero Buffalo Bill Cody. Titles such as *The Crimson Trail, Buffalo Bill's Grip; or, Oath-Bound to Custer*, and *Buffalo Bill's Gallant Stand; or, The Indian's Last Victory* featured Cody avenging the General by taking "the first scalp for Custer," which happened to be just about exactly what happened. Upon hearing of the general's death, the showman left his Wild West show to join the cavalry in pursuit of the hostile Indians. On July 17, 1876, he killed a Cheyenne warrior named Yellow Hair and scalped him, then held the bloody tangle of hair and skin up for all to see. Cody was soon performing the five-act drama *The Red Right Hand; or, Buffalo Bill's First Scalp for Custer* regularly to sellout crowds.

Other parts of the story were instrumental in mythologizing Custer, but none more so than the battle itself. The loss of a complete unit at the hands of a vastly superior force is an irresistible iconic element. The 183-man garrison defending the Alamo against 2,500 Mexican soldiers . . . Roland and his Franks, the rear guard of Charlemagne's army, ambushed at Roncesvalles . . . Leonidas and his 300 Spartans fighting back the Persian army at Thermopylae . . . the foolhardy Charge of the Light Brigade at Balaclava . . . These and others have assured their participants legendary status forever. Custer's Last Stand fit right in with that roster of epic defeats—all, of course, in the name of a noble cause. Most Americans, even to this day, think of it as one of our nation's transcendent moments. Historically speaking, the battle was a minor one and decided nothing. There are probably a hundred, even two hundred, battles in our nation's history that were strategically more important or more costly, but the Last Stand achieved mythic status because its peculiar mix of elements and personalities combined to fill an integral need of the American consciousness and how we view ourselves. As long as Americans find meaning and validity in it, the myth will survive— and thrive—at the expense of history.

Custer was, perhaps more than any other individual, the symbol of America's Manifest Destiny. He protected the railroad as it forged its way through the West; he invaded the sacred Black Hills and discovered the ore that began a gold rush of white men into the area; and he did as much as anyone to subdue the "noble red man"—or at least so it seemed to the American public. It didn't matter that he lost

One of the more persistent stories that cropped up almost immediately after the Battle of the Little Bighorn was that of the lone survivor—a man who rode with Custer but somehow survived to view Custer's final moments and live to tell the tale.

his life in the Plains Indians' greatest triumph. Because of his name recognition and renown as the nation's best-known Indian fighter (though there were others more deserving of that accolade), almost a century later in the 1960s, Custer became the symbol of all the wrongs that white America had visited on the Indian people. As he was no more guilty of genocidal white oppression than most of the army's other leaders—and less guilty than, say, John Chivington of the infamous Sand Creek Massacre—the common modern-day Indian-country bumper sticker "Custer Died For Your Sins" is striking but inaccurate. Custer may have died for our collective sins, but he also died for our dreams, our hopes, and our vision of America.

Can we have both symbols? Perhaps. For better or worse, the Villain is doomed to perpetual second-place status behind the Hero. This has little to do with reality, and much to do with something deep within ourselves that is unutterable and unalterable—and because we prefer to think of ourselves as heroic rather than barbaric. "Print the legend," said a newsman in John Ford's elegiac western, *The Man Who Shot Liberty Valance*, and despite tarnishing, that's what will happen. The image of Custer and his vastly outnumbered soldiers heroically fighting to the death touches white Americans—and many others—too deeply for any mitigating facts to change. We can admire the courage of Custer and his men on the Little Bighorn and at the same time lament the personal hubris and governmental wrongheadedness that got them there.

Finally, there is this: Every country, every people with a history of war has at its core a belief, a confidence, in its ultimate bravery—that no matter the enemy or the odds, our people and our culture will be defended, if necessary, to the death. Custer's Last Stand symbolizes and reinforces that supreme courage for Americans. The man died; the legend will endure as long as there is an America.

Facing page: **First Scalp for Custer**

Upon hearing of events on the Little Bighorn, Custer's old scout-turned-showman, Buffalo Bill Cody, closed his Wild West show, and marched with General George Crook and his troops in search of revenge. On July 17, 1876, Cody killed Cheyenne warrior Yellow Hair and scalped him. Always one to capitalize on his own fame, Cody was soon performing the five-act drama The Red Right Hand; or, Buffalo Bill's First Scalp for Custer *regularly to sellout crowds.*

Below: **Stereoscope view of the "Burial Place of Gen. Custer and His Brave Men"**

136. Burial Place of Gen. Custer and His Brave Men, Wyoming.

Bibliography

Ambrose, Stephen E. *Crazy Horse and Custer: The Parallel Lives of Two American Warriors*. New York: Doubleday, 1975.

Asay, Karol. *Gray Head and Long Hair: The Benteen-Custer Relationship*. Paris, Texas: privately printed, 1983.

Barnett, Louise. *Touched By Fire*. New York: Henry Holt, 1996.

Bradley, James H. *The March of the Montana Column: A Prelude to the Custer Disaster*. Norman, Oklahoma: University of Oklahoma, 1961.

Brady, Cyrus Townsend. *Indian Fights and Fighters*. New York: McClure, Philips & Company, 1904.

Brown, Dee. *Bury My Heart at Wounded Knee: An Indian History of the American West*. New York: Holt, Rinehart & Winston, 1971.

Colbert, David, ed. *Eyewitness to America*. New York: Random House, 1997.

Connell, Evan S. *Son of the Morning Star: Custer and the Little Big Horn*. San Francisco: North Point Press, 1984.

Custer, Elizabeth B. *Boots and Saddles; or, Life in Dakota with General Custer*. New York: Harper and Brothers, 1885.

Custer, George A. *My Life on the Plains; or, Personal Experiences with Indians*. New York: Sheldon and Company, 1874.

Darling, Roger. *General Custer's Final Hours*. Vienna, Virginia: Potomac-Western Press, 1992.

———. *A Sad and Terrible Blunder—Generals Terry and Custer at the Little Bighorn: New Discoveries*. Vienna, Virginia: Potomac-Western Press, 1993.

Dippie, Brian W. *Custer's Last Stand: The Anatomy of an American Myth*. Missoula, Montana: University of Montana, 1976.

Dixon, Joseph K. *The Vanishing Race: The Last Great Indian Council*. Garden City, New York: Doubleday, 1913.

Dodge, Colonel Richard Irving. *Our Wild Indians: Thirty-three Years' Personal Experience Among the Red Men of the Great West*. Hartford, Connecticut: A. D. Worthington and Company, 1885.

Donnelle, A. J. *Cyclorama of Custer's Last Battle, Or: The Little Big Horn*. Boston: Boston Cyclorama Company, 1889.

Du Bois, Charles G. *The Custer Mystery*. El Segundo, California: Upton and Sons, 1986.

———. *Kick the Dead Lion: A Casebook of the Custer Battle*. Reprint, El Segundo, California: Upton and Sons, 1987.

Dunn, J.P. *Massacres of the Mountains: A History of the Indian Wars of the Far West*. New York: Harper and Brothers, 1886.

Ennis, Ben. *Bloody Knife: Custer's Favorite Scout*. Revised edition. Bismarck, North Dakota: Smoky Water Press, 1994.

Finerty, John. *War-Path and Bivouac; or, The Conquest of the Sioux*. Chicago: Donohue & Henneberry, 1890.

Fougera, Katherine Gibson. *With Custer's Cavalry*. Caldwell, Idaho: Caxton Printers, 1940.

Fox, Richard Allan Jr. *Archaeology, History, and Custer's Last Battle: The Little Big Horn Reexamined*. Norman, Oklahoma: University of Oklahoma Press, 1993.

Frost, Lawrence. *Custer Legends*. Bowling Green, Ohio: Bowling Green University Popular Press, 1981.

Graham, W. A. *The Custer Myth: A Source Book of Custeriana*. Harrisburg, Pennsylvania: Stackpole, 1953.

———. *The Story of the Little Big Horn: Custer's Last Fight*. New York: Century, 1926.

Gray, John S. *Centennial Campaign: The Sioux War of 1876*. Fort Collins, Colorado: The Old Army Press, 1976.

———. *Custer's Last Campaign: Mitch Boyer and the Little Big Horn Reconstructed*. Lincoln, Nebraska: University of Nebraska, 1991.

Hammer, Kenneth M. *Custer in '76: Walter Camp's Notes on the Custer Fight*. Provo, Utah: Brigham Young University, 1976.

Hardorff, Richard G. *The Custer Battle Casualties, II*. El Segundo, California: Upton and Sons, 1999.

———. *Hokahey! A Good Day to Die! The Indian Casualties of the Custer Fight*. Spokane, Washington: Arthur H. Clark, 1993.

———. *Lakota Recollections of the Custer Fight: New Sources of Indian-Military History*. Spokane, Washington: Arthur H. Clark, 1991.

Hatch, Thom. *Custer and the Battle of the Little Bighorn: An Encyclopedia*. Jefferson, North Carolina: McFarland and Company, 1997.

Hofling, Charles K. *Custer and the Little Big Horn: A Psychobiographical Inquiry*. Detroit: Wayne State University Press, 1981.

Horn, W. Donald. *Portrait of a General*. West Orange, New Jersey: Don Horn Publications, 1998.

———. *Witnesses for the Defense of General George Armstrong Custer*. Short Hills, New Jersey: Horn Publications, 1981.

Hunt, Frazier, and Robert Hunt. *I Fought With Custer: The Story of Sergeant Windolph, Last Survivor of the Battle of the Little Big Horn*. New York: Charles Scribner's Sons, 1947.

Jackson, Donald. *Custer's Gold*. New Haven, Connecticut: Yale University Press, 1966.

Keegan, John. *Warpaths: Travels of a Military Historian in North America.* London: Hodder and Stoughton, 1995.

Kidd, James H. *Personal Recollections of a Cavalryman with Custer's Michigan Cavalry Brigade in the Civil War.* Ionia, Michigan: Sentinel Press, 1908.

Liddic, Bruce R., ed. *I Buried Custer: The Diary of Pvt. Thomas W. Coleman, 7th U.S. Cavalry.* College Station, Texas: Creative Publishing Company, 1979.

Lowie, Robert H. *Indians of the Plains.* New York: McGraw-Hill, 1954.

Mahon, Michael G. *The Shenandoah Valley, 1861-1865: The Destruction of the Granary of the Confederacy.* Mechanicsburg, Pennsylvania: Stackpole, 1999.

Marquis, Thomas B. *She Watched Custer's Last Battle.* Hardin, Montana: privately printed, 1933.

Merington, Marguerite, ed. *The Custer Story: The Life and Intimate Letters of General George A. Custer and His Wife Elizabeth.* New York: Devin-Adair, 1950.

Michno, Gregory. *Lakota Noon: The Indian Narrative of Custer's Defeat.* Missoula, Montana: Mountain Press Publishing, 1997.

———. *The Mystery of E Troop: Custer's Gray Horse Company at the Little Bighorn.* Missoula, Montana: Mountain Press Publishing, 1994.

Miles, Nelson A. *Personal Recollections and Observations of General Nelson A. Miles.* Chicago: Werner, 1896.

Miller, David Humphreys. *Custer's Fall: The Indian Side of the Story.* New York: E. P. Dutton, 1957.

Monaghan, Jay. *Custer: The Life of General George Armstrong Custer.* Boston: Little, Brown, 1959.

Neihardt, John G. *Black Elk Speaks: Being the Life Story of a Holy Man of the Oglala Sioux.* Lincoln, Nebraska: University of Nebraska, 1961.

Nevin, David. *The Old West: The Soldiers.* New York: Time-Life Books, 1974.

Pratt, Fletcher. *Civil War in Pictures.* New York: Henry Holt, 1955.

Reedstrom, E. Lisle. *Custer's 7th Cavalry: From Fort Riley to the Little Big Horn.* New York: Sterling, 1992.

Reynolds, Arlene. *The Civil War Memories of Elizabeth Bacon Custer.* Austin, Texas: University of Texas, 1994.

Robinson, Charles M., III. *Bad Hand: A Biography of General Ranald S. Mackenzie.* Austin, Texas: State House Press, 1993.

———. *A Good Year to Die: The Story of the Great Sioux War.* New York: Random House, 1995.

Rosenberg, Bruce A. *Custer and the Epic of Defeat.* University Park, Pennsylvania: Pennsylvania State University Press, 1974.

Russell, Don. *Custer's Last; or, The Battle of the Little Big Horn in Picturesque Perspective; Being a Pictorial Representation of the Late and Unfortunate Incident in Montana.* Fort Worth, Texas: Amon Carter Museum, 1968.

Scott, Douglas D., and Richard A. Fox Jr. *Archaeological Insights into the Custer Battle: An Assessment of the 1984 Field Season.* Norman, Oklahoma: University of Oklahoma Press, 1987.

Scott, Douglas D., Richard A. Fox Jr., Melissa A. Connor, and Dick Harmon. *Archaeological Perspectives on the Battle of the Little Bighorn.* Norman, Oklahoma: University of Oklahoma, 1989.

Scott, Douglas D., P. Willey, and Melissa A. Connor. *They Died with Custer.* Norman, Oklahoma: University of Oklahoma, 1988.

Stewart, Edgar I. *Custer's Luck.* Norman, Oklahoma: University of Oklahoma, 1955.

Stewart, Edgar I., and Jane R., eds. *The Field Diary of Lieutenant Edward Settle Godfrey . . . .* Portland, Oregon: The Champoeg Press, 1957.

Urwin, Gregory J. W. *Custer Victorious: The Civil War Battles of General George Armstrong Custer.* Rutherford, New Jersey: Fairleigh Dickinson University, 1983.

Utley, Robert M. *Cavalier in Buckskin: George Armstrong Custer and the American Frontier.* Norman, Oklahoma: University of Oklahoma, 1988.

———. *Custer and the Great Controversy: The Origin and Development of a Legend.* Pasadena, California: Western Lore Press, 1980.

———. *Custer Battlefield: A History and Guide to the Battle of the Little Big Horn.* Handbook 132. Washington, D. C.: National Park Service, 1988.

Utley, Robert M., ed. *Life in Custer's Cavalry: Diaries and Letters of Albert and Jennie Barnitz, 1867-68.* New Haven, Connecticut: Yale University Press, 1977.

Utley, Robert M., and Wilcomb E. Washburn. Indian Wars. New York: American Heritage, 1977.

Van de Water, Frederic F. *Glory-Hunter: A Life of General Custer.* Indianapolis, Indiana: Bobbs-Merrill, 1930.

Vaughn, J. W. *With Crook at the Rosebud.* Harrisburg, Pennsylvania: Stackpole, 1956.

Viola, Herman J. *Little Bighorn Remembered: The Untold Indian Story of Custer's Last Stand.* New York: Times Books, 1999.

Wert, Jeffry D. *Custer: The Controversial Life of George Armstrong Custer.* New York: Simon and Schuster, 1996.

Weymouth, Lally. *America in 1876.* New York: Vintage Books, 1976.

Wheeler, Colonel Homer W. *Buffalo Days.* Indianapolis, Indiana: Bobbs-Merrill, 1925.

Whittaker, Frederick. *A Complete Life of Gen. George A. Custer.* New York: Sheldon and Company, 1876.

Index

About the Author

Photo by Phillip Esparza

Jim Donovan is the author of several other books. He is a literary agent in Dallas, Texas, where he lives with his wife, Judith, and his daughter, Rachel.